# Search Patterns

*Peter Morville and Jeffery Callender*

Beijing · Cambridge · Farnham · Köln · Sebastopol · Taipei · Tokyo

Search Patterns
by Peter Morville and Jeffery Callender

Published by O'Reilly Media, Inc., 1005 Gravenstein Highway North, Sebastopol, CA 95472.

O'Reilly books may be purchased for educational, business, or sales promotional use. Online editions are also available for most titles (*http://my.safaribooksonline.com*). For more information, contact our corporate/institutional sales department: (800) 998-9938 or *corporate@oreilly.com*.

**Editor:** Simon St.Laurent     **Indexer:** Julie Hawks

**Production Editor:** Rachel Monaghan     **Cover Designer:** Karen Montgomery

**Copyeditor:** Amy Thomson     **Interior Designer:** Ron Bilodeau

**Proofreader:** Rachel Monaghan     **Illustrators:** Jeff Callender and Nellie McKesson

**Printing History:**

January 2010: First Edition.

ISBN: 978-0-596-80227-1

[TI]

# Advance Praise for Search Patterns

"*Search Patterns* is a playful guide to the practical concerns of search interface design. It contains a bonanza of screenshots and illustrations that capture the best of today's design practices and presents a fresh perspective on the broader role of search and discovery."

—Marti Hearst
Professor, UC Berkeley, and author, *Search User Interfaces*

"It's not often I come across a book that asks profound questions about a fundamental human activity, and then proceeds to answer those questions with practical observations and suggestions. *Search Patterns* is an expedition into the heart of the Web and human cognition, and for me it was a delightful journey that delivered scores of insights."

—Dave Gray
Founder and chairman, XPLANE

"Search is swiftly transforming everything we know, yet people don't understand how mavens design search: by stacking breadcrumbs, scenting widgets, and keeping eyeballs on the engine. I urge you to put your eyeballs on this unique and important book."

—Bruce Sterling
Writer, futurist, and cofounder, The Electronic Frontier Foundation

"As one who searches a lot (and often ends up frustrated), I found *Search Patterns* to be a revelation."

—Nigel Holmes
Designer, theorist, and principal, Explanation Graphics

"*Search Patterns* is a fabulous must-have book! Inside, you'll learn the whys and wheres of practically every modern search design trick and technique."

—Jared Spool
CEO and founder, User Interface Engineering

# Contents

# Preface

**Chapter 1**
## Pattern Recognition

- Defines search
- Explains why it's important
- And why it's so difficult

**Chapter 2**
## The Anatomy of Search

- Describes the users, interface, engine, content, and creators
- Explores broader contexts of knowledge management and information architecture

**Chapter 3**
## Behavior

- Explains user psychology and classic patterns of behavior
- Introduces the elements and principles of interaction design

**Chapter 4**
## Design Patterns

- Illustrates the design patterns
- Includes tons of examples, especially web and mobile

**Chapter 5**
## Engines of Discovery

- Covers browsing, serendipity, discovery, and answer engines
- Even more interfaces, including kiosk and interactive TV

**Chapter 6**
## Tangible Futures

- Methods and deliverables
- Semantic webs, social search, personalization, and beyond
- Futuristic search scenarios

# Pattern Recognition

*" The future isn't just unwritten—it's unsearched. "*
—Bruce Sterling

In astronomy, *averted vision* is the art of seeing distant objects by looking to their periphery. It works by shifting responsibility from cones, which sense color and fine detail, to rods, which detect motion and help us to juggle, play chess, and see in the dark. This form of peripheral vision can be practiced. Observers often report a gain of three to four magnitudes. It's a powerful reminder that sometimes we must look away to see.

This book will test our ability to juggle multiple visions of search and discovery. We will look to the center by describing a pattern language for search that explains user psychology and behavior, embraces emerging technologies and rich interaction models, and illustrates repeatable solutions to common problems. We will explore the edges by studying cool tools that help users ask, browse, learn, share, visualize, and understand.

This juggling act is necessary if we are to pursue both incremental improvement and radical innovation. In today's world of intense competition and rapid change, both are essential. Search applications demand an obsessive attention to detail. Simple, fast, and relevant don't come easy. Success requires extraordinary focus in research, design, and engineering, yet you can't test and tweak your way from Google to Twitter. Time and again, the future of search is invented beyond the borders of its category.

And, search has a future. Search is not a solved problem. Indeed, search is a wicked problem of terrific consequence. As the choice of first resort for many users and tasks, search is a defining element of the user experience. It changes the way we find everything from answers, articles, and advertising to products, people, and places. It shapes how we learn and what we believe. It informs and influences our decisions, and it flows into every nook and cranny. Search thrives within and across myriad contexts and channels. Web, e-commerce, enterprise, desktop, mobile, social, and real time are just a few of its classifications. Search is among the biggest, baddest, most disruptive innovations around. It's a source of entrepreneurial insight, competitive advantage, and impossible wealth.

Unfortunately, it's also the source of endless frustration. Search is the worst usability problem on the Web. It's held that title for many years. We find too many results or too few, and most regular folks don't know where to search, or how. From enterprise to e-commerce, user needs and business goals are obstructed by failures in findability.

And the news doesn't improve when you change the channel. Mobile search is a mess, kiosks are worse, and interactive television remains the lonely domain of the early adopter. Your average couch potato isn't quite ready to trade his remote control for a search box.

**Figure 1-1.** *A manager explains why search stinks*

Of course, pundits claim we'll solve search soon with artificial intelligence, information visualization, personalization, and the Semantic Web, but this fabled future never arrives. Search remains as noisy and irregular as language and communication. Vendors hawk their wares to IT executives who understand business and technology but turn a blind eye to user experience. Content stakeholders perfect their publishing workflow only to bury their crown jewels behind firewalls and within tightly controlled information silos. Design teams work hard to make search simple, but lack the skills and tools to ensure relevance and speed. Once in a while, the stars do align and real solutions emerge, but in most organizations and applications today, bad search remains an inconvenient truth.

And even when search works well, it can always be improved. Even Google is only good enough until something better comes along. In search, innovation is a forced move. It's not easy, but it's not impossible. It is important. And that is the reason for this book. We want to make search better. Or, to be more precise, we want to inspire you to make search better. But first, we had better define what it is that we seek to improve.

# UNDERSTANDING SEARCH

The way we define a problem or frame a question shapes how we and our colleagues understand, answer, and act. An overly narrow formulation leads to tunnel vision, and we're oblivious to all but the obvious. But stray too far from the center, and we lose our focus while trying to boil the ocean. The best strategy is to avert and revert, juggling ideas, patterns, gaps, and oddballs in the periphery without losing sight of the goal.

## THE BOX

In search, the first ball in the air is a box. It's the iconic symbol of search and a great place to start. Enter a keyword or two, and you're good to go.

Figure 1-2. *The iconic search box*

The box comes in all colors, shapes, and sizes. It sports a variety of buttons and labels. It appears as a feature of sites, browsers, applications, and operating systems, and it's found across channels and within all forms of interactive media. The box has grown so familiar it now lives in our heads like Plato's perfect circle. We recognize it as a box, even when it's not.

Figure 1-3. *When is a box not a box?*

Of course, each box has its secrets. How can I search? What's being searched? Its affordance tells us little about language and scope. Are we querying the text of Twitter or the metadata of music? And can we simply enter keywords or must we speak Boolean? The answers are revealed by context and experience. On Flickr, we know we seek images, but we must learn how and why to query by tag and filter by interestingness.

Figure 1-4. *There are many dialects in the language of search*

Similarly, the behavior of each box is revealed only by interaction (or word of mouth). As we begin to type, autocomplete offers to save time and typos, while autosuggest serves up Best Bets and related topics. Or, we can highlight a phrase in Firefox, drag and drop it into the search bar, and query a custom search engine using only our mouse.

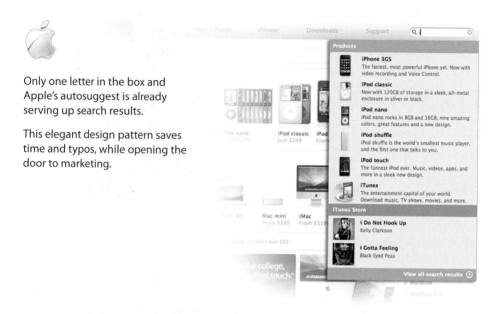

Only one letter in the box and Apple's autosuggest is already serving up search results.

This elegant design pattern saves time and typos, while opening the door to marketing.

Figure 1-5. *Apple's colorful version of autosuggest*

iPhone users soon learn the rhythm of tap and type, understanding that the box has become subject to touch. Or we simply raise our phones to our ears and speak our search, relying on Google Mobile to derive what we want from who we are, where we stand, and what we say. No buttons. No typing. No clicks. Our identities, locations, and voices form a new kind of query that has us searching (and thinking) outside the box.

# Google

Google uses the iPhone's onboard accelerometer to support gestural interaction.

So, we can lift the phone to our ears and speak a search.

Like placing your hands under a tap to turn on the water, this is the type of smart design that "dissolves in behavior."

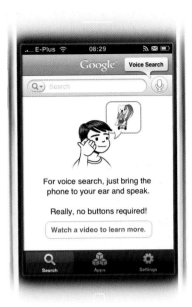

*Figure 1-6. Google Mobile with Voice Search on the iPhone*

Further reflection is inspired by the interplay between input and output. Often, the results are links and snippets, but sometimes they are answers to questions. If you ask nicely, Google will reply with weather forecasts, stock quotes, traffic maps, and sports scores.

*Figure 1-7. Google presents structured results for special query types*

You can track packages, perform calculations, and visualize data. This is where things get interesting. The box isn't limited to search—it's also a command-line interface that affords power and flexibility to users in the know. It's a calculator. It's a communicator. It's a universal remote control. The box is a boundary object that links design, engineering, and marketing. We must work together to see what it can do.

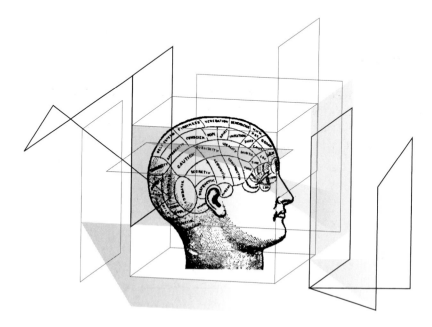

Figure 1-8. *The thinking box*

The only limit is ourselves. In the prophetic words of William Gibson, "The box was a universe, a poem, frozen on the boundaries of human experience."[1]

## THE GOAL

Yet, if we keep our eyes on the box, we may lose sight of the goal. After all, search is first and foremost about *findability*. We search to find objects and answers. We seek to find (and re-find) pages, people, places, products, and facts. The archetypal search is a quick lookup that leads from query to results to found object. It serves as a navigation shortcut that speeds our way from here to there. Search is the means to an end.

---

1 *Count Zero*, William Gibson (Ace).

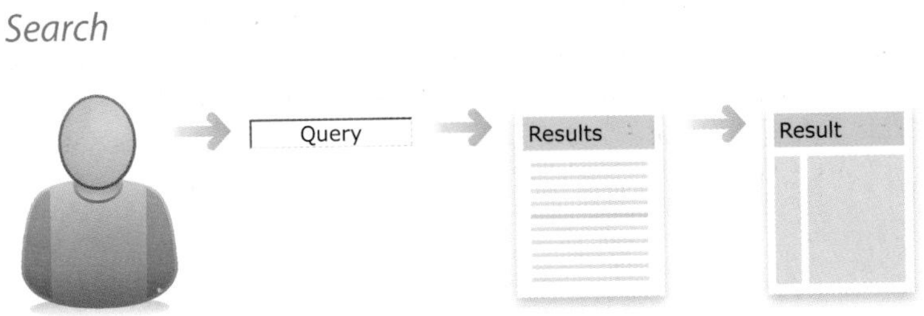

*Search*

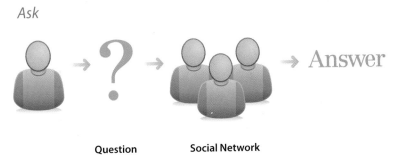

**Figure 1-9.** *We search to find results*

Of course, search isn't the only way we find. We often ask family, friends, and colleagues. Where are my keys? What's the best way to the market? What's that URL? Sometimes we ask professionals. Is there a great vegetarian restaurant near the hotel? Can you help me find a good book about global warming? What's this fungus on my foot?

*Ask*

**Question**          **Social Network**

**Figure 1-10.** *We ask to find answers*

Our strategies for asking are often situated by time and place. There are questions at dinner and questions for the doctor. Yet, we increasingly displace these questions by searching for answers in a box. In fact, the line between ask and search is fuzzy, defined mostly by distinctions of syntax and semantics. A query is simply a question without the ornament of natural language. When we ask and search, we seek to find. That is the goal.

Sometimes we don't need to ask; the answers find us. In our everyday experience, we are inundated by information. News, spam, facts, and gossip flow into our attention through a mesh of channels, networks, subscriptions, and feeds. Our relationships, memberships, identity, and location form an ongoing query against a universal dataset.

*Filter*

**Figure 1-11.** *We use filters so the right stuff finds us*

We rely on people, tools, algorithms, and impatience as filters. Still, junk gets in. On the other hand, we often find what we need without leaving the house or lifting a finger.

We also browse to find. We wander aisles, scan shelves, sort papers, open folders, click links, flick photos, and shuffle songs. This takes time and invites serendipity. We never know what we may stumble upon. Browsing evokes a sense of place. There are trails, edges, signs, maps, and landmarks that test our wayfinding skills. As a spatial experience, browsing is unique, and yet many of its most worn paths lead directly to and from search.

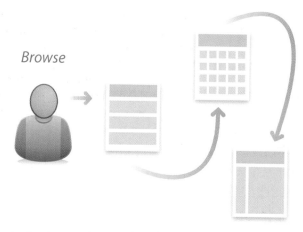

**Figure 1-12.** *Browsing involves wandering and wayfinding*

In fact, we move fluidly between modes of ask, browse, filter, and search without noting the shift. We scan feeds, ask questions, browse answers, and search again.

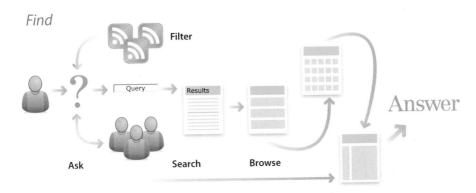

Figure 1-13. *We flow between modes*

All these modes should be on the table when designing for findability. Each is but one tactic in support of a goal. Rather than prescribing tools and tasks, we must aim for (and beyond) the searchers' intent. What do they want? What do they need? But, before accepting our mission, it's worth challenging the objective, because search isn't only about finding.

As any concierge or librarian will avow, their jobs aren't simply to answer questions. They first conduct exploratory conversations or reference interviews to better under-stand what we want and why. A hotel guest who asks for a local area map may be on her way to a restaurant that closed last month. The concierge can identify a suitable alternative and call ahead for reservations. A library patron who wants an old issue of *Consumer Reports* may be buying a new car, and he may not know the library provides access to an online database of reviews and ratings. The librarian can help jumpstart his search. Oftentimes, due to a gap in knowledge or language, the searcher isn't able to ask the right question.

That's why search at its best is a conversation. It's an iterative, interactive process where we find we learn. The answer changes the question. The process moves the goal. Search has the power to suggest, define, refine, cross-sell, upsell, relate, and educate. In fact, search is already among the most influential ways we learn. It's trusted and relied upon by millions of people a day. Search is the world's most popular teacher. As designers, we must expand our vision beyond finding to incorporate learning. And we can't stop there.

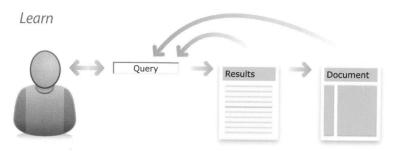

**Figure 1-14.** *In search, we find we learn*

Search also has the ability to enhance understanding. A search engine results page (SERP) is a custom map that's built in response to a query. It's how we see what we've found. This potential is best realized in faceted search, where the selective presentation of metadata fields and values serves as a table of contents to the result set. But it's also evident in the way Google surfaces diverse content types and related queries. And we're finally starting to see real progress at the intersection of information visualization and search, where rich results can provoke exploration, insight, and understanding.

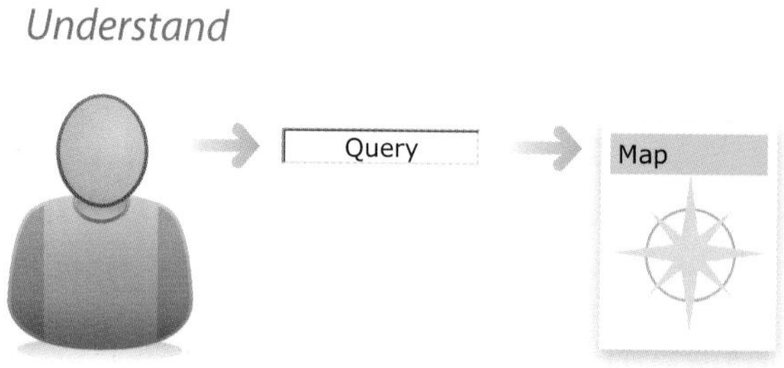

*Understand*

**Figure 1-15.** *Search helps us understand what we've found*

Of course, these quests to find, learn, and understand rarely occur in isolation. Search isn't always a solo sport. We search on behalf of other people. We search with other people. We crowdsearch with Twitter and Mechanical Turk, distributing our queries (as whispers or shouts) to a networked community of searchers and solvers. Search can be a social experience in which we share goals, queries, and results. As designers, we must strive to support collaborative discovery. We must help people to search together.

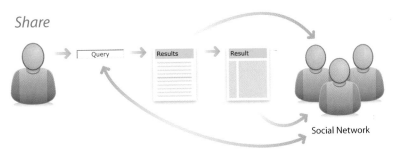

Figure 1-16. *We often search together*

The goals of users may warrant other acts. While print, save, and share are most common, a variety of tasks may be integral to the process. Increasingly, on result pages, we can play music, watch videos, buy products, update calendars, and call contacts.

Figure 1-17. *Users deserve actionable results*

The promise is particularly rich in mobile, but each channel offers unique possibilities for integrating useful features into actionable results. Search is not just about findability. We search to learn, understand, share, and act. As designers, when we focus on goals, the challenge becomes exhilarating (and scary), because the end of search is a moving target.

## THE ENGINE

A more traditional way to define search is by its software. Buy the engine, then figure out what it's good for. This can put search in a straightjacket. How often have we been told the engine can't handle that content type or index multiple sites or rank by popularity or respond in less than a lifetime? So search fails because all too often, if it's not easy, it's not possible. When technology precedes requirements, the user experience suffers.

This approach also leads to solutions in search of problems. Remember when relevance scores were all the rage? Your first result is 78% relevant. What the heck did that mean? Why did companies clutter their results with useless trivia? Because it was a default. The engine made it easy. Similarly, most natural-language interfaces, flashy result visualizations, and autocategorizers are simply high-tech hammers in search of nails.

Then again, hammers do have their uses. A tool in the hand is worth two in the box. Hammers extend our reach and amplify force. They push buttons and break down doors. Similarly, engines can do more than search. For instance, there's an engine called Evri, shown in Figure 1-18, that appears in the *Washington Post*'s website. At the end of each article, readers can learn more about relevant people, organizations, and topics.

Evri uses a map of people, places, and things to connect users with related objects.

While there's an engine behind Evri, their motto is:

search less. understand more.

**Figure 1-18.** *Evri's suggestions for an iPhone article*

Using Evri, readers don't search, they simply follow a link. But search is the engine that powers this experience. The same is true on e-commerce sites where most links are queries against the product catalog and the analytics database. Even when we browse, we search.

This reframing of search has produced a whole new generation of discovery tools and recommender systems. Last.fm, Pandora, Ambiently, and StumbleUpon are search without the box. We click, jump, and vote. Keywords are displaced by hearts and thumbs.

We also open the door to innovation by sharing the search API. The *New York Times*, for instance, allows third parties to create tools for exploring its database. With over 13 million articles, 35 fields per article, and support for faceted search, this is an amazing playground for developers to build anything from custom link lists and remote search widgets to complex visualizations. New applications can expand their audience and clever mashups can expand their minds by showing how news can be reimagined.

In search, innovation through collaboration is smart strategy. Emerging technologies from disparate categories can suddenly inject search with new possibility. For instance, in the subset of machine learning known as pattern recognition, our devices are learning to recognize and analyze faces, footfalls, gunshots, speech, text, images, and data. Sensors and algorithms combine to detect threats, track trends, and identify anomalies. And software agents tell us what topics to search. It's truly difficult for us humans to stay current, so we need to keep many eyeballs on the engine without losing sight of the goal.

## THE DISCOVERY OF COLOR

The spectral colors of red, orange, yellow, green, blue, indigo, and violet are produced by light of a single wavelength, and are all visible to the human eye, except for indigo, which most people can't distinguish. Isaac Newton included indigo so the number of colors would match the number of known planets, notes in a major scale, and days in a week. Of course, any list of colors is arbitrary in a spectrum of infinite variation. Colors are categories we use to explain what we see and, in the case of ultraviolet and infrared, what we don't. We even have imaginary colors like octarine, the eighth color, an elusive spectral mix that's hard to describe and impossible to perceive. That's the thing about color. Try describing a rainbow or a sunset to a blind person or ask a synesthete to tell you about the sound of blue or the color of Monday.[2] Most of us are unable to fully accept or appreciate this cross-sensory perception. We have to see to believe.

---

2 *Synesthesia* is a neurological phenomenon in which stimulation of one sensory or cognitive pathway leads to automatic, involuntary experiences in a second pathway, as when the hearing of a sound produces the visualization of a color. People who report such experiences are known as *synesthetes*.

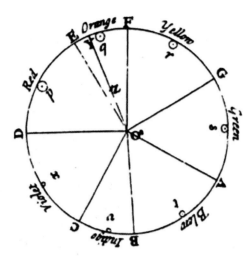

Figure 1-19. *Newton's color wheel, showing the colors correlated with musical notes and symbols for the known bodies within the solar system*

The same holds true in search. We have a number of well-established categories: web, e-commerce, enterprise, desktop, mobile, social, and real time. Within each category, we embrace a set of proven technologies, business models, user behaviors, and best practices. We are mostly blind to the chaotic yet colorful array of search startups and design patterns dancing on the horizon. There are so many possible futures for search and discovery, and it's hard to discern good ideas from bad. In the 1990s, folks laughed at a startup named GoTo and the absurd idea of paid search. Meanwhile, people raved about PointCast. Push was the next big thing. Until it wasn't. We've made many mistakes and it's tempting to give up. Why engage a future so unevenly distributed? It's safe to be a skeptic, so we stay within our category and copy the competition. We test and refine, we celebrate incremental improvement, and we laugh at the latest big idea for reinventing search. "What a joke! That'll never work." Again, we have to see to believe.

Inevitably, this insularity leads to a category error. We omit a key feature because "that won't fly in the enterprise." We miss the next Twitter because "that's not search." This is why it's so important to look beyond our borders. The enterprise can learn from e-commerce. We must simply adjust for different constraints, metrics, and goals. It's equally vital to reorganize. Like colors, our categories are arbitrary by nature. We organize to understand, and we must reorganize to see anew.

For instance, there's clear value in naming the primary colors of search. This classification provides a quick way to reference the major categories and key players. It helps us explain the market dynamics and business strategies behind divergent search solutions. And, as the color wheel illustrates beautifully, it offers a glimpse of the brilliant diversity of search.

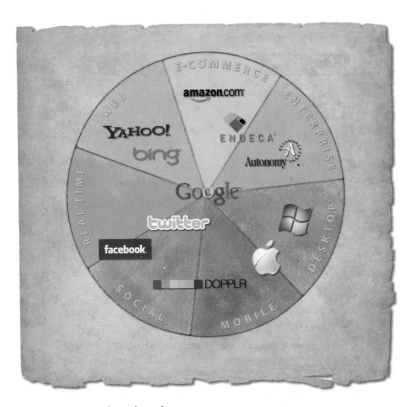

**Figure 1-20.** *The primary colors of search*

This is not a pure organization. On the contrary, it's a loose grab bag of context, purpose, and platform. Yet it still belies the true chaos of the marketplace for discovery. We Yahoo! on the iPhone and use Google Desktop to query web history. We search social conversations threaded over applications, channels, languages, and time zones for embedded links that connect to any media. Search won't fit cleanly on a color wheel. In fact, these categories reveal more about the history of search than its future.

Today, search is best imagined as an artist's palette, as shown in Figure 1-21. The mixing of colors has begun. Lovely hues and shades exist outside the categories. We can see them better when we shuffle our ways of organizing. For instance, there are riches within the niches of format.

In images, we find the photo facets of Getty, the interestingness of Flickr, and the visual recognition of Like.com, which lets us search and shop by color, shape, and pattern.

In music, Songza turns the results interface into a jukebox, Midomi lets us search by singing, and Last.fm spins our personal channel into a melody of social discovery.

In video, Everyzing unlocks the vault with its speech-to-text translation technology, while NetFlix, Hulu, and Boxee search together and apart for the future and end of TV.

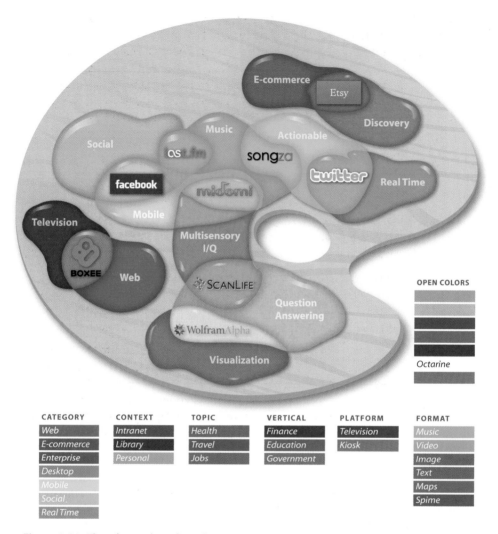

**Figure 1-21.** *The infinite colors of search*

We can also organize by subject and industry, taking a close look at search verticals like health, travel, and real estate. Or we can sort by approach, focusing on text analytics, clustering, question answering, personalization, visualization, or rich results. Each organizational scheme adds combinatorial possibilities to our palette. Desktop search is social and personal. It's not about the desktop. Music is mobile. There's video in every vertical. The potential for cross-fertilization is huge. Diversity is the inexorable result of search.

As designers, we can learn from each color and combination. Many ideas work once, or never, but there are patterns of behavior and design that bridge contexts. In this book, that's our target: we will aim to explore core concepts and best practices by studying examples drawn from within and between contexts. And we will repeatedly try to escape the category. What kinds of information and objects are unsearchable? What, if anything, will never be subject to search? What can we learn from asking, browsing, and filtering? Where is the boundary between search and unsearch? To think outside the box, we will search beyond the periphery. Sometimes we must look away to see.

## ELEPHANT IN THE ROOM

Of course, whether it's a wretched beggar on the sidewalk or a pink elephant on the dinner table, sometimes we look away to ignore. We avoid taboo topics and inconvenient truths by focusing on small distractions. It's a tactic that's at home in the kitchen and the corner office. And it's often at work in IT, where search is an elephant we prefer to duck.

Let's face it: search is a wicked problem with no definitive formulation, considerable uncertainty, and complex interdependencies. Stakeholders have divergent goals and radically different world views. Requirements are incomplete, contradictory, and everchanging. Search is both a project and a process. It's a problem that's never solved.

And that's not the half of it. Our organizations are woefully unprepared to tackle search. We lack the team and the technology. Unlike Google, most firms aren't structured to manage the high-tech, step-changing, cross-functional, user-centered challenge. There are too many hyphens. As a hybrid of engineering, marketing, and design, search creates too many openings for missing links. As a complex adaptive system that's sensitive to scale, search is a mystery that morphs over time. Search isn't just wicked, it's downright dangerous. Why risk your career (and your weekends) on a problem that's so intractable?

Especially when it's also invisible. That's right. Search is an elephant that hides in plain sight because executives lack the right radar. Many in management don't realize the role search plays in defining the user experience. They fixate on the home page, they fuss about look and feel, and they care about the content. They may even fume about findability, but they are easily distracted or misled because they really don't understand search.

"What problem?"

Figure 1-22. *Ducking the elephant*

So, it's safest to keep search small. Buy a brand, defer to defaults, don't ask questions, maintain plausible deniability, and be ready with a response. The speed is subject to security. We had to choose fast or safe. It's too hard to make it easy. We can't afford the cost. The results are relevant in theory. Our problem is the users. They use the wrong keywords. But, it's not worth much attention, because our users mostly don't search.

We underfund and understaff search, and its poverty becomes a self-fulfilling prophecy. In many contexts, expectations have been crushed. Users don't search now since search failed then. Sometimes they browse. Often they bail. They abandon online for phone and email. This regress to more costly channels is bad for business. It's also sad for society.

## The Sadness of Search

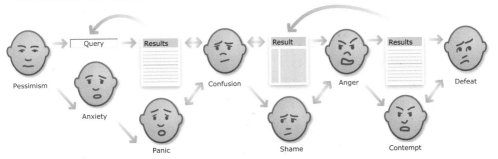

Figure 1-23. *Poor search is bad for business and sad for society*

Every increase in search costs diminishes our quality of life. Poor search wastes time like a crooked street sign that sends us in the wrong direction. It erodes trust, derails learning, and confuses decisions. It makes us blame ourselves. And therein lies the problem. For most people, search is sufficiently advanced technology that it's indistinguishable from magic. We don't know what to expect or who to blame. We certainly can't see what's missing. Our response can be emotional. We suffer. We feel sadness, shame, anger, and disgust. Sometimes we soldier on, unhappy but resolute. Often we surrender. We simply fail to search. We live uninformed without seeing what we miss, for the cost of the unsearched is an unseen drag on commerce and culture, as invisible as it is incalculable.

## The Joy of Search

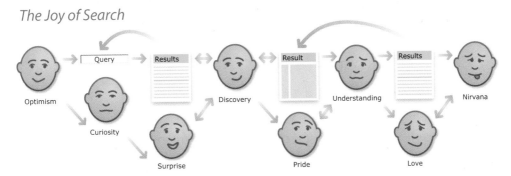

Figure 1-24. *Search can be a source of information and inspiration*

It doesn't have to be this way. When we design with our users in mind, search can be an engine of inspiration and joy. We find what we want. We discover what we need. We stimulate our minds and recover our memories. We feel surprise, wonder, amusement, and pride. Search is a core life activity that engages both intellect and emotion. It has the power to change a life or save a business. For designers, search is a grand challenge, an elephant we should not duck. We can succeed at search. We just need courage and vision.

# A MAPMAKER'S MANIFESTO

In this book, our taste for rhetoric and imagery may run amok. Adding color to the message can occasionally obscure its meaning. That is not our intent. So, for the sake of clarity, here are our beliefs and principles in plain language:

1. Search is a problem too big to ignore.
2. Browsing doesn't scale, even on an iPhone.
3. Size matters. Linear growth compels a step change in design.
4. Simple, fast, and relevant are table stakes.
5. One size won't fit all. Search must adapt to context.
6. Search is iterative, interactive, social, and multisensory.
7. Increments aren't enough. Even Google must innovate or die.
8. It's not just about findability. It's not just about the Web.
9. The challenge is radically multidisciplinary.
10. We must engage engineers and executives in design.
11. We can learn from the past. Library science is still relevant.
12. We can learn from behavior. Interaction design affords actionable results.
13. We can learn from one user. Analytics is enriched by ethnography.
14. Some patterns, we should study and reuse.
15. Some patterns, we should break like a bad habit.
16. Search is a complex adaptive system.
17. Emergence, cocreation, and self-organization are in play.
18. To discover the seeds of change, go outside.
19. In science, fiction, and search, the map invents the territory.
20. The future isn't just unwritten—it's unsearched.

OK, so a rhetorical flourish or two infiltrated our manifesto. What can we say? They're sneaky little buggers! But our aim is clear. We are passionate about search. We believe it's far more interesting and important than most people realize. We aspire to get the design right and the right design through refinement and reinvention. We don't have all the answers. Neither do you. But as writers and designers, we are inventing the future of experience and discovery. We are the mapmakers. Together, we can make search better.

## APOPHENIA REDUX

In *Pattern Recognition*, William Gibson defined *apophenia* as "the spontaneous perception of connections and meaningfulness in unrelated things."[3] It's an old term, coined by a psychologist in 1958, that enjoys new life in our fast, flat world. Apophenia is a type-1 error, a false positive caused by excess sensitivity. Most neurologists agree this condition exists in everyone. It's a natural bias of the human mind. We search for patterns to explain and anticipate change. On occasion, we see a new trend. Invariably, we confuse signal for noise. Apophenia is a symptom of madness and creativity. When artists, entrepreneurs, and autistic savants spot new patterns in music and markets, they walk the fine line between crazy and genius. It's a line we should all walk more.

Of course, there's value to be had in mining old patterns, as the architect Christopher Alexander eloquently intimated in *The Timeless Way of Building*:

> " *There is one timeless way of building.*
>
> *It is thousands of years old, and the same today as it has always been.*
>
> *The great traditional buildings of the past, the villages and tents and temples in which man feels at home, have always been made by people who were very close to the center of this way.* " [4]

In his quest for "the quality without a name," Alexander developed a practical way to catalog patterns of behavior and design. His pattern language offered a structured method for identifying and illustrating repeatable (optimal) solutions to common problems.

---

3 *Pattern Recognition*, William Gibson (Penguin).

4 *The Timeless Way of Building*, Christopher Alexander (Oxford University Press).

## Window Place (180)

Everybody loves window seats, bay windows, and big windows with low sills and comfortable chairs drawn up to them.

May be part of:
- Entrance Room (130)
- Zen View (134)
- Light on Two Sides (159)
- Street Windows (164)

May contain:
- Alcoves (179)
- Low Sill (222)
- Built-In Seats (202)
- Deep Reveals (223)

*A Pattern Language*
*Christopher Alexander et al.*

Figure 1-25. *A pattern language for architecture*

This framework has been embraced in a variety of fields from ecology and education to engineering and design. Recently, we've enjoyed access to pattern libraries that help us create more useful, usable, and desirable software and interfaces. Yahoo!, in particular, has done a brilliant job of sharing patterns and code with the wider community (Figure 1-26).

Patterns embed wisdom, yet we should mind whose patterns we trust. Not all are created equal. To design well, we must understand how patterns fit together and relate to a context of use. A pattern in one scene is a problem in the next. If we aspire to innovate, we must dare to break the mold. Nobody said the timeless way was easy.

> *We are searching for some kind of harmony between two intangibles: a form which we have not yet designed and a context which we cannot properly describe.* [5]

---

5 *Notes on the Synthesis of Form*, Christopher Alexander (Harvard University Press).

Developer Network Home    Help

## YAHOO! DEVELOPER NETWORK

Design Pattern Library

Yahoo! Developer Network > Design Pattern Library > Reputation

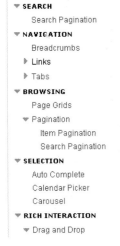

**USER NEEDS TO**

▼ **SEARCH**
  Search Pagination
▼ **NAVIGATION**
  Breadcrumbs
  ▶ Links
  ▶ Tabs
▼ **BROWSING**
  Page Grids
  ▼ Pagination
    Item Pagination
    Search Pagination
▼ **SELECTION**
  Auto Complete
  Calendar Picker
  Carousel
▼ **RICH INTERACTION**
  ▼ Drag and Drop

# Reputation

### Problem Summary

A person participating in a social structure expects to develop a reputation and hopes for insight into the reputations of others, but each designed model of participation and reputation embodies its own set of biases and incentive structures. Balancing these forces determines in large measure the success or failure of a social system.

### Solution Patterns

The Competitive Spectrum
The designer needs to match the reputation system to the community's degree of competitiveness.

Named Levels
Participants in a community need some way to gauge their own personal development within that community.

Numbered Levels
Participants in a community need some way to gauge how far they've progressed within that community.

Figure 1-26. *Yahoo!'s pattern library*

In this task, past performance may impede future results. Therein lies the paradox of prediction. We must look back to see ahead, but as Mark Twain noted, "History doesn't repeat itself—at best it sometimes rhymes." To envision the next stanza, we might take a page from e.e. cummings, the mud-luscious poet of unconventional syntax:

   " *Understand the rules. Then, break them with intent.* "

That's the problem with the future of search. The prophets don't understand. Neither do the investors, executives, and journalists who swallow their sermons whole. Often, they don't know how search works. They rarely grok the complexity of software development, and they certainly don't understand how user psychology and behavior are related to the success or failure of search applications. So, apophenia runs rampant. It's hard to keep track of all the paradigm shifts and Google killers, especially when they fail so fast. Ironically, spin notwithstanding, the official future of search—artificial intelligence with a dash of information visualization—hasn't changed in decades. Most search startups just add new wrinkles to an old face. We're stuck on the original *Star Trek*, seeking technological singularity and the agents of tomorrow in a rusty rearview mirror. It's like the signs outside British pubs that promise "Free Beer Tomorrow" forever.

There is a way to break the stalemate. We can unlock the game of improve versus innovate. We can forsake the tyranny of the OR for the genius of the AND.[6] The key is vision. We must focus on the fine detail of stable patterns at the center, while keeping an eye on emerging technologies at the periphery. We must know what we see and where to look.

*"I'm searching for my keys."*

Figure 1-27. *Drunk under the lamp post*

That's the aim of this book. It's a lens for refraction and reflection. It's a microscope, a telescope, and a kaleidoscope. By studying patterns and surveying trends, we will learn to improve and innovate. And by adding to our tools and palette, we will make search more visible and vibrant for ourselves and for those without vision. This book is a practical guide to the future, a colorful map to frameshift, and a doorstop to boot. We wrote it because the box is reshaping the globe right now. It's a topic both timely and timeless. Search is a core life activity, as ancient in its form as the trees and hills, and as our faces are. We must discover its patterns and break them with intent. Let's get cracking!

---

6 *Built to Last*, Jim Collins and Jerry Porras (Harper).

# The Anatomy of Search

*" How can a part know the whole? "*
—Blaise Pascal

In anatomy, we divide to understand. We dissect the whole to study its parts. We identify internal organs and map their relationships. As a major branch of biology, anatomy reflects both the power and the limits of specialization. For we must not allow our focus on form and structure to distract us from function or blind us to context. Anatomy can't tell us how the mind works. It can't reveal the sublime experience of vision. And it certainly can't predict the behavior of an ant colony or a stock market. These complex adaptive systems exhibit macroscopic properties of self-organization and emergence. Not only is the whole greater than the sum of its parts, but it's also different. It's a territory off the map. And yet, our simple models have value, for they offer us a very good place to start.

Our map to search features five elements: users, creators, content, engine, and interface. Like any map, it hides more than it shows. It's deceptive by design. It shifts attention from software and hardware to the elements of user experience. Our plan is to study each element without losing sight of the whole. We must know enough about the technology to understand what's difficult and what's possible. But we need not become intimately familiar with load balancing, pattern matching, and latent semantic indexing. That's why we have specialists. Instead, we'll study the components and context in sufficient detail to inform strategy and design. We'll survey the terrain in search of the big picture. So, let's start at the very beginning with the users for whom we design.

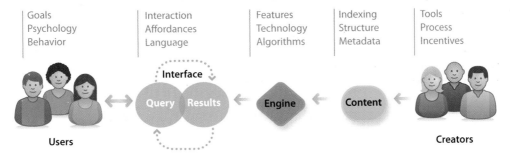

**Figure 2-1.** *The anatomy of search*

# USERS

There's a lot we can learn about our users. *Demographics* cover income, age, and gender. *Psychographics* reveal values, attitudes, and lifestyle. *Technographics* segment user populations by their adoption of tools and software. Some of this data is useful for designing better search systems. Much of it is not. It's all too easy to stuff a treasure chest with worthless facts and figures. Organizations do it all the time. The key to profitable user research is knowledge. We must know enough to ask the right questions. We must understand the basics of user psychology and behavior as they relate to the type of system we plan to build. We require a conceptual framework that lets us focus on the pivotal questions that make the difference in design. We need a scalpel, not a hatchet.

For instance, we know the *paradox of the active user* is a constant in search. Most people refuse to read the manual, personalize the system, or prepare a strategy before they begin, despite evidence that such initial "presearch" improves overall efficiency. We enter two or three keywords and we *GO*. We're seduced by the illusion of speed. It's only when we find we're lost that we check a map or ask for help. Of course, some users love manuals, while others must study them in training. But for most users in most contexts, this paradox is active. Knowing this helps us to excise unfit questions and designs.

Another timeless topic is the question of precision versus recall. Do our users care more about finding *only* the relevant results or *all* the relevant results? In search design, the two are inversely related. Like kids on a seesaw, when one goes up, the other comes down. High precision generally means we miss some of the good stuff, while high recall forces us to sift through the good, the bad, and the ugly, except when a better algorithm or a richer interaction model lets us "bend the board" by amplifying the signal without adding noise. Either way, it's worth asking, especially since the answer may signal a pivot point where user and business goals diverge. In e-commerce, for example, a user may want to find a specific product as quickly as possible, whereas a vendor may allow for more noise, hoping that cross-selling will spur an impulse buy. It's critical to identify and manage this predictable source of tension in the user experience.

We should also consider expertise with respect to search in general and the domain in question. Let's say we're building a search application for health and medicine. Will most users (or our most important users) be familiar with medical terminology? And how about their digital literacy? Are they fluent or fumbling? It's a common mistake to conflate these two types of mastery. People assume that good doctors are good searchers, but that's not true at all. Their magic has limits. In most domains, there are wizards and muggles who can and can't search, and each group needs different support. Knowing the relative strengths and weaknesses of our target audiences is a key to good design.

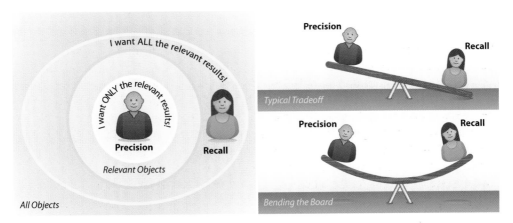

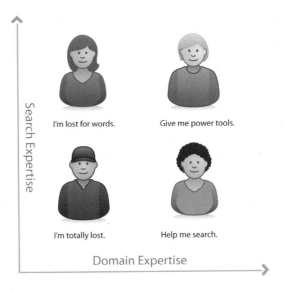

Figure 2-2. *The relevance seesaw*

Figure 2-3. *Expertise types*

Type of search is another key variable. There's a big difference between the simple lookup of known-item search and the dynamic learning of exploratory search. Google's got lookup down. Fast, simple, relevant. If you know what you want, Google will find it in less than a second. It's so fast, we use it for navigation, running queries even when we know the URL. But if you're unsure what you need, Amazon offers a better model. Faceted navigation plus tools for recommendation help us learn. Search becomes an iterative, interactive experience where what we find changes what we seek. While each type begins in a box, the types diverge by process and goal. Many systems must support both. To design well, we must think carefully about how and where to strike the right balance.

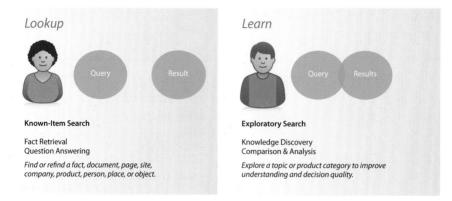

Figure 2-4. *Search modes*

Of course, we must also consider platform, purpose, and context of use. Are we designing for desktops, laptops, televisions, kiosks, or mobiles in motion? The iPhone's small screen and soft keyboard place new limits on search, especially when it's jiggling in your palm in the back of a taxi cab in downtown Berlin at midnight. On the other hand, its multisensory I/O tears down old walls. When we integrate a microphone, speaker, GPS, accelerometer, magnetometer, and a multitouch interface, we redefine what's feasible in search. The whole may not recognize the sum of its parts. Design must respond to context. That's why it's good to ask where your users will be when they need you.

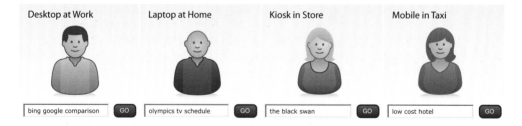

Figure 2-5. *Context of use*

Finally, we should seek to balance the qualities of the user experience. In mobile, search must be useful and usable. Simple, fast, and relevant wins the day. But in music, search begets desire. Cover Flow makes it OK to look, while Pandora tempts us to buy. In government, accessible and credible are tops, but in business, search must be found, and real results add value to the bottom line. In each context, we must identify which qualities our users and organizations value, and then design with these priorities in mind.

**User Experience Honeycomb:** *Searcher's Edition*

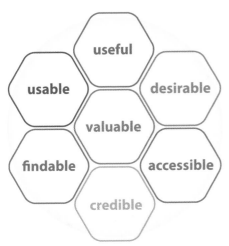

**Useful**
Is it useful? Is search the right solution? Will it help our users achieve their goals?  And, given the state of technology, should we revisit our goals? Can search be more?

**Usable**
Is it easy to use with maximum efficiency and minimal error? Are there affordances for novice and expert searchers? Are there gentle slopes to support learning?

**Desirable**
Is it satisfying to use? Does it make people want to search? Does it embody the values and identity of your brand? Does search leverage the power of emotional design?

**Findable**
Can users find your site? Can they find their way around your site? Can they find your content despite your site? Is search aligned with search engine optimization?

**Accessible**
Will it work for all users? Are features and results accessible to blind and visually impaired users? Can people search from a wide variety of platforms and browsers?

**Credible**
Does the design inspire trust? Do the order and display of results convey authority? Will users believe that the top results are the best or most popular or most relevant?

**Valuable**
What is the value of search? Does it build the bottom line or advance the mission? Is the user experience aligned with strategy? Can search confer competitive advantage?

Erasable
How do these qualities interact? Which are most and least important to search? What have we missed? Go ahead. Erase a few. Add your own. This is only a place to start.

Figure 2-6. *Qualities of the searcher's experience*

That's a lot to know about users, and we've only just nicked the surface. We could study their patterns of behavior or explore how to apply user research methods to search. But we'll save those topics for later. For now, let's interact with the interface.

# INTERFACE

The classic view of search implies a two-step process in which a user types a query into the box and is presented with a list of results. The interface bisects input and output. It's a delightfully simple model. It's also increasingly wrong. Today, the speed of search and the richness of interaction blur the lines between query and results. Subsecond responses let us search, scan results, skim content, and search again. Autocomplete asks for only a letter or two before it suggests queries and recommends results, and faceted navigation rewards us with a map that is the territory. Query, results, content, and interface flow into one another in a journey that changes the destination. This intertwingled reality means we have to work together. Designers, engineers, and creators are all responsible. It also means we can't rely on old patterns for the interface. We must think outside the box.

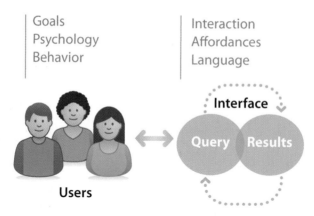

**Figure 2-7.** *The interface includes query and results*

To begin, we might consider affordance. What are the real and perceived action possibilities? This simple query submits readily to the maxim of the Five Ws (and one H), as memorialized in a poem by Rudyard Kipling:

> " *I keep six honest serving-men*
>
> *(They taught me all I knew);*
>
> *Their names are What and Why and When*
>
> *And How and Where and Who.* " [1]

In journalism, this maxim is useful for getting the full story. In search, it's helpful for creating and analyzing whole interfaces and their (perceived) affordances.

---

1 *Just So Stories*, Rudyard Kipling (Puffin).

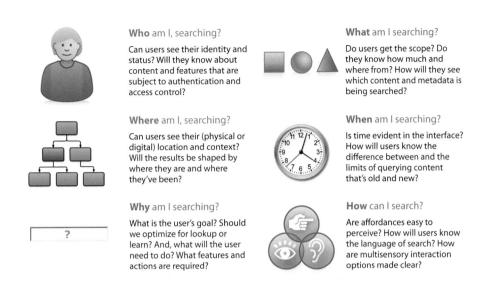

**Who** am I, searching?

Can users see their identity and status? Will they know about content and features that are subject to authentication and access control?

**What** am I searching?

Do users get the scope? Do they know how much and where from? How will they see which content and metadata is being searched?

**Where** am I, searching?

Can users see their (physical or digital) location and context? Will the results be shaped by where they are and where they've been?

**When** am I searching?

Is time evident in the interface? How will users know the difference between and the limits of querying content that's old and new?

**Why** am I searching?

What is the user's goal? Should we optimize for lookup or learn? And, what will the user need to do? What features and actions are required?

**How** can I search?

Are affordances easy to perceive? How will users know the language of search? How are multisensory interaction options made clear?

Figure 2-8. *The Five Ws (and one H)*

The most obvious questions are *what* and *how*. What am I searching? How can I search? An interface that fails to answer simply fails. But it's also worth asking *who, where, when,* and *why*. These questions stretch our minds. They encourage us to think more holistically about the interface and how it separates and binds together input and output.

Which returns us to results. The search engine results page or SERP, as pictured in Figure 2-9, is among the most complex and important challenges to design. We'll study the concepts, elements, and design patterns in detail later. For now, suffice it to say that whether the results are too few, too many, or just plain wrong, this interface addresses a pivotal point in the user experience. The surprise of results opens a gap in the paradox of the active user. It's at this critical juncture that people know they are lost and admit they need help. It's a teachable moment in which real humans (even grown men) will actually accept advice, read maps, customize parameters, and choose carefully from a list of next steps. It's a tiny gap, and it closes fast. We must be ready with the right design empowered by the right technology, because behind every great search interface is an engine that delivers results.

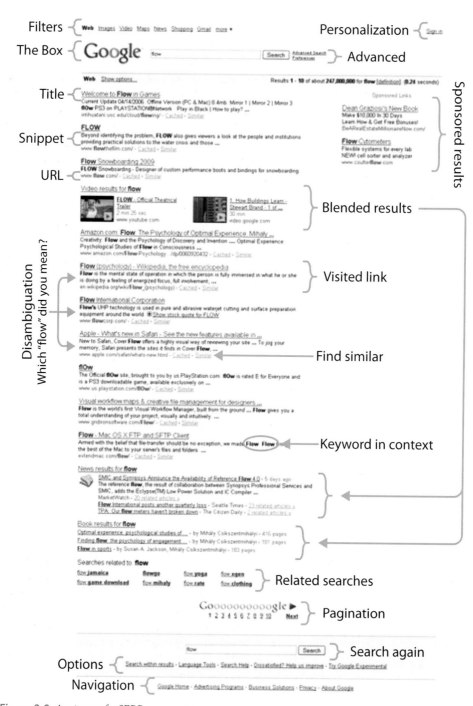

Figure 2-9. *Anatomy of a SERP*

# ENGINE

Most of us have no idea how stuff works. We are surrounded by technology sufficiently advanced that it's indistinguishable from magic. We can't possibly know everything, so we specialize. And outside our niche, we satisfice. We learn just enough to get by. As users, we rely on mental models to tame our technology. These simple explanations and visualizations, often derived via metaphor, keep us safe and efficient. For instance, we know how to use a toaster: insert bread, lower handle, wait for the pop. We also know not to chase a missing earring with a fork before unplugging the toaster, since the electricity that flows like water from the wall up the cord to the appliance might rush up the fork and zap us. This mental model is not technically correct, but it does keep us alive. Now, if we want to be better users, we may need better models. How should we adjust the timer for the second batch of toast? What if the kitchen is hot or cold? To answer, we must know the basics of capacitors and resistors, or we can learn by trial and error. If we aspire to build a better toaster, we'll need even richer models and a deep understanding of users, technology, and how they (might) interact in the real world.

Figure 2-10. *Anatomy of a toaster* [2]

The same is true in search. Users have no idea how search works. Most designers aren't sure, either. We treat search as a black box. We rely on engineers to define parameters for input and output. And we miss opportunities to make search better. It's time to change. Designers must learn more about engines, indexes, and algorithms. And we should reach out and collaborate with engineers. We should engage them in the process of design and inject ourselves into search engine selection and configuration. Our expertise reveals what's desirable. Their skill and insight shows what's possible. By working together, we can identify risks, invent new solutions, and make search better.

---

2 Dave Gray hosts a wonderful set of toaster diagrams as part of his visual thinking collection at *www.flickr.com/photos/davegray/collections/72157600017554580/*.

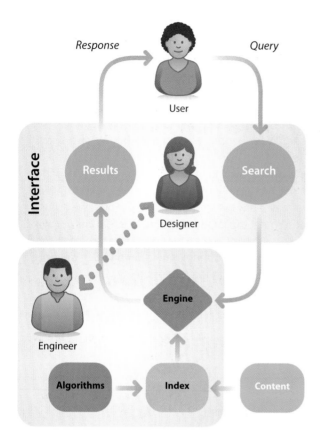

Response    Query

User

Interface

Results    Search

Designer

Engineer

Engine

Algorithms → Index ← Content

### Learning + Collaboration

Designers must learn more about how search works. And, we should collaborate more effectively with engineers.

**Engine**

Designers must be involved in selecting a search vendor and application. User needs and the information architecture strategy should inform requirements analysis.

**Index**

Indexing defines which content and metadata fields are searchable and how. Federated searching across multiple indexes may slow performance.

**Algorithms**

Results can be ranked by relevance, date, format, popularity, etc. Tuning the engine for your mix of content, user needs, and business goals makes all the difference.

**Interface**

Engineers should help with brainstorming. They may see possibilities for improving or reinventing search applications that are invisible to designers and executives.

*Figure 2-11. Learning together*

Ideally, the evaluation of search applications is preceded by development of an information architecture strategy that puts user needs and business goals ahead of the features and limitations of software products. As we'll discuss later in this chapter, the information architecture positions search within a broader context, allowing us to see how the multiple modes of ask, search, browse, and filter can work together. This blueprint clarifies priorities with respect to what we will actually need from search. Of course, more often than not, firms put the cart before the horse. There's usually plenty we can do to work with and around any engine, but there's no harm in hoping for blue skies.

On the other hand, it's irresponsible to design an information architecture without practical consideration of technology, staff, and cost. A limited budget may suggest a hosted solution such as Google Custom Search. An open source solution like Solr may be right if there's sufficient in-house technical expertise. If not, the quick install and easy configuration of Microsoft Search Server may appeal. If the user experience is mission-critical to your business, a high-end information access platform (like Endeca or Autonomy) that manages more than search may be the way to go. Each class and product imposes limits on what's possible and what's easy. For this reason, the architecture should be informed by analysis of the realistic outcomes of search engine selection.

A designer can add further value during the software selection process by building on the blueprint. Organizations often cover the bases in terms of technology and finance but fail to press vendors on exactly what will be required to support their unique mix of features and content. A typical checklist may include the following:

*System architecture*
> Formal description of the hardware and software components, including crawlers, indexers, data models, and query parsers.

*Performance*
> How many simultaneous queries are supported? What's the maximum number of sources? How about the size of the data repository?

*File formats*
> What types of content and data (e.g., HTML, PDF, mySQL) are supported? Can the system handle both structured and unstructured data?

*Integration*
> Is there a standards-based Web Services API for embedding search functionality in other sites and software? Is there a list of available connectors?

*Access control*
> Does the system support multiple levels of access for different user types and individuals? How does it manage privacy and security?

*Features*
> How does the system handle full text and metadata? Does it support Boolean operators, wildcards, stemming, stop words, phrase and proximity searching, and spellcheck? What algorithms are used for ranking? What are the options for query refinement? Can results be saved, printed, and shared?

*Implementation*
> What sort of expertise is required for installation, configuration, and maintenance? How does the vendor handle training and support?

*Pricing model*
> Is the product priced by data or activity volume, CPUs, features, and/or number of unique applications? How about support, maintenance, and professional services fees? What's the total cost of ownership?

*Vendor credentials*
> How long has the vendor been in business? How are they positioned in the market? Can we see their financials and customer references?

These are all necessary questions, but they're also insufficient. Because there's so much ground to cover, it's easy to lose sight of the goal. The designer's role is to repeatedly refocus attention on the user experience. A supplemental checklist that's informed by an information architecture strategy and empathy for the user might include:

*Speed*

What will it take to ensure subsecond response in the real world? It's worth asking this question early and often. Don't take "slow" for an answer!

*Relevance tuning*

How are results ranked? Is it possible to adjust the settings to allow for popularity, content type, date, and diversity?

*Navigation and filtering*

Is it easy to customize sort order and limit options? Is there native support for faceted navigation? Is it fast?

*Federated search*

How does the system handle the simultaneous search of multiple databases or indexes? What is the impact on speed? Is it possible to merge several indexes into one to dramatically improve performance?

*Linguistic toolset*

Is there support for thesaurus integration and crosswalking between vocabularies? How about autocategorization and entity extraction?

*Search analytics*

What tools are provided for measuring and understanding user behavior? Is there an API that supports sharing and repurposing of this data?

These lists are just a way to start the conversation between designers and engineers. We must also track emerging technologies, because what's possible in search keeps shifting. Because these changes come from so many directions, we need all the eyeballs we can get. By working together, we're likely to make better purchase decisions, identify the long-term costs associated with continuous improvement, and generate insights that lead to innovation in search and discovery. Plus, we'll learn a little more about how stuff works.

# CONTENT

The design of a search application is defined by its content. A social network, an image library, and a mixed media database merit totally different solutions. For starters, the availability (or lack thereof) of full text and metadata shapes the *what* and *how* of search.

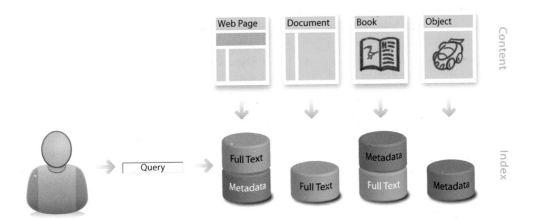

**Figure 2-12.** *Relative value of text and metadata*

Consider, for instance, these four content types and their associated search scenarios:

*Web page*

A web page includes both visible content and off-the-page HTML tags for title, description, and keywords. The first appears in the browser's title bar and the second in the snippets of search results. All of these embedded metadata tags are indexed by web search engines, but keywords are not weighted heavily, due to spam concerns (e.g., keyword stuffing). Inbound links from other pages and the collective navigation, search, and post-query behavior of many users deliver rich streams of external metadata. In the case of hypertextual web pages, engines can rely on this full spectrum of content and metadata to discern meaning, which is why Google appears to work like magic.

*Document*

On a typical underfunded intranet, search engines must rely solely on the contents of technical reports, white papers, spreadsheets, presentations, marketing materials, and online forms to reveal their own *aboutness*. The absence of structured metadata precludes faceted navigation, and full-text relevance-ranking algorithms struggle with the heterogeneity of multiple content types and lengths. There are limits on how much meaning can be "automagically" extracted from natural language, which is why intranet search is so bad.

*Book*

In books, Amazon draws upon a rich index for search and navigation. While lacking Google's database of inbound links, Amazon enjoys everything else: full-text content, social data, and behavioral metadata. Plus, it has oodles of formal, structured metadata to enable filtering, sorting, personalization, and faceted navigation, which is why Amazon integrates search and browse so well.

*Object*

In the absence of full text, metadata is often a forced move. In cars, investment in controlled vocabularies and structured metadata is required, and search is limited to fields like make, model, price, and fuel efficiency. In images, Flickr found a way to share the cost with tags, notes, descriptions, and comments that power findability surprisingly well. Nontext objects present major challenges to search, which is why they inspire so much innovation.

Of course, we need not be satisfied with the status quo. Since complexity of the information retrieval challenge increases exponentially with linear increases in volume, we know the most dramatic way to improve performance is to search less content.

**Content**
Shrink the search space by removing the ROT.

Designer    Creator

**Metadata**
Provide filters so users can slice up the search space.

User    Designer

*Figure 2-13. To search better, search less*

So, early in the design process, it's worth asking two questions. First, can we shrink the search space by removing *ROT*, content that's redundant or outdated or trivial? By crafting a content policy that defines what's in and out, then rigorously weeding their collections, organizations are often able to cut what's searched by half. Second, can we add metadata fields that let users slice content into smaller sections? Even a massive article database becomes manageable when users can limit searches by topic and date.

These questions invite consideration of context. What is the business model? What can we afford to invest? How much content are we talking about? Where does it come from? How quickly will it grow or change? And what about metadata? Is its creation inherent to the publishing process? Should we hire librarians? Or can software handle entity extraction and autocategorization? When we look at content, it's easy to get technical. After all, this is the domain of information technology. But we should also get social, because search is a network that includes and inspires the creators behind the content.

# CREATORS

In the early days, adventures in search required vertical integration and an entrepreneurial spirit. During the 1960s, pioneers of the first information retrieval networks couldn't rely on existing infrastructure—they had to design the whole system. Hardware, software, networks, protocols, algorithms, content and metadata creation, user training, and billing were part and parcel of the job. In contrast, today we enjoy a robust infrastructure that affords specialization. Modern search tools and technologies allow us to concentrate on customization. Unfortunately, they also let us be lazy. It's all too easy to focus on interface design without challenging our creativity by reimagining content and context.

That's why the biggest innovations in search come from outside the category. Wikipedia serves as a case in point. By reinventing the encyclopedia as a collaborative work, Jimmy Wales made a huge improvement to search. While Google is the means, Wikipedia is the end. We Google to find the Wikipedia article. It's inevitably at the top of results. The cocreators of Wikipedia invest time in writing and editing because they know their articles will be found via Google. Wikipedia is a tool that embodies process and incentives. It motivates millions of users to become creators of content and metadata, in part by sharing its analytics in detail. In addition to overall statistics, we can see data about each article, user, and creator. This transparency is conducive to widely distributed competition and collaboration. It's a success story in which knowledge management and search combine to foster a participation economy where the reward is recognition. It's also a repeatable solution to a common problem. This social design pattern, which enlists users as cocreators and coorganizers, has been copied liberally by entrepreneurs under the banner of Web 2.0. And while they may have already grabbed the low-hanging fruit, it's a really big tree that has much to offer search.

Designers of search applications must no longer accept content in its current state. It's time to shake the tree. Questions we should ask include:

- Who are the current (and potential) creators of content?
- How can we motivate them to improve quality and quantity?
- What tools and processes will make publishing faster and easier?
- How can we enlist users in content creation and organization?
- How can we share analytics to inspire both use and cocreation?

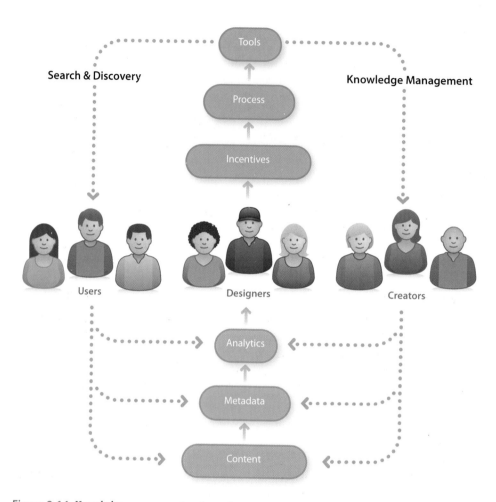

Figure 2-14. *Knowledge management and search*

Search is social. This realization invites us to think, not only about information and technology, but also about people. Of course, we shouldn't stop there. It's a mistake to believe the source of all creation is human. Sensors are creators, too. Increasingly, networks of sensors allow us to query temperature, pollution, traffic density, and product availability. Our mobile devices know their own locations, which changes how we search and how we are found. How can we improve the quality and quantity of content and metadata to advance user and business goals as they relate to search and discovery? Who (and what) are all the potential creators? These are the questions we ask when we see that knowledge management is part of search. And, upon finding we're engaged in the holistic design of complex adaptive systems, we understand that we need a new map.

# CONTEXT

The late Harvard professor Alan Watts, in a lecture on Eastern philosophy, used the following analogy to introduce the subject of context:

> " *If I draw a circle, most people, when asked what I have drawn, will say I have drawn a circle or a disc, or a ball. Very few people will say I've drawn a hole in the wall, because most people think of the inside first, rather than thinking of the outside. But actually these two sides go together—you cannot have what is 'in here' unless you have what is 'out there.'* "

A similar reaction occurs when we hear the word "search." We tend to think inside the box. We forget that the search "in here" is made possible by the structure "out there." That's why the design of search applications is best framed by information architecture. We need a framework that positions search within the broader context of organization, navigation, personalization, and discovery. We need maps that reveal the paths, edges, districts, nodes, and landmarks of the user experience. We also need blueprints that show the complex relationships between form, function, structure, process, and goal.

Let's consider, for instance, a website. Most sites don't need search. Browse is sufficient for the vast majority of simple sites operated by individuals and small firms. A solid taxonomy with clear categories and labels is enough. Perhaps a sitemap or index is useful to complement navigation, but search is unnecessary. In fact, adding search may be downright dangerous, since most queries will lead to nowhere. However, when success leads to big business, the architecture must change. Browse fails to scale. For this reason, the sites of large organizations often exhibit the following problems:

*Fragmentation*
Fragmentation into multiple sites, domains, and identities becomes a huge distraction. Users don't know which site or subsite to visit for which purpose, and the lack of consistent, intuitive intersite search and navigation makes it hard to find content without knowing source and location.

*Findability*
Users can't find what they need from the home page, but that's only the start of the problem. Most users don't come through the front door; they enter via a web search or a deep link, and are confused by what they do find. Even worse, most potential users never use the site, because many of its resources aren't easily discoverable via Google or other web search engines.

So, for most people, the content is invisible. You can't use what you can't find. And for those who do find the site, the experience is frustrating. These problems are common for good reason. By necessity, in large organizations, different groups are responsible for different pages, sites, and services. Over time, in the absence of a master plan, the structure devolves into a chaotic sprawl reminiscent of the Winchester Mystery House, a well-known California mansion that was under construction continuously for 38 years.

**The Winchester Mystery House**

The house was once the home of Sarah Winchester, the widow of gun magnate William Winchester.

According to legend, after her daughter and husband both died young, Sarah consulted a psychic who told of a curse upon the family intended to avenge all the lives taken by the guns they made.

Sarah was told to build a home for herself and the fallen spirits, and if she ever stopped building, she too would die. The house is reportedly haunted.

*Figure 2-15. The Winchester Mystery House*

The Winchester Mystery House has 160 rooms, 40 staircases, 467 doorways, and no blueprint. It's not an unattractive house, and the view from any individual room isn't particularly unusual or overwhelming, but it's virtually impossible to grasp the whole or to find your way.

When a site reaches this scale, it's time to look for the levers. Since we all must live within limits, it's imperative that we identify strategic opportunities where leverage affords the most positive impact for the effort and investment. In the context of websites, three key areas often emerge as powerful fulcra with the potential to move mountains: the portal, search system, and destination objects, as shown in Figure 2-16.

In a moment, we'll explore these fulcra in the context of a big organization and its website. We'll examine the unique potential of each lever. But first, it's vital to recognize their interdependent nature. The information infrastructure of objects and search serves as a necessary foundation for a successful, sustainable, user-centered portal. As users shift between modes of browsing, searching, and reading, proper integration enables a sense of flow. The whole is greater than the sum of its parts. A concept map, as shown in Figure 2-17, can help us to realize this big picture. The goal is to capture the key elements so we can begin to discuss how they relate. In *The Back of the Napkin*, Dan Roam defines what he calls the garage-sale principle: "Everything looks different when we can see it all at once."[3] An early stage concept map is an effective way to put all the parts on the table.

---

3 *The Back of the Napkin*, Dan Roam (Penguin Books).

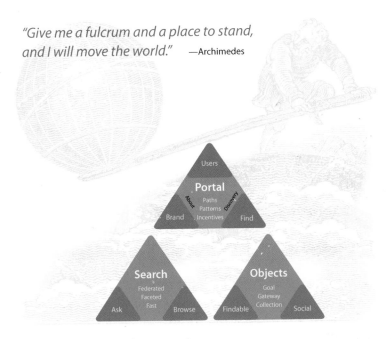

*"Give me a fulcrum and a place to stand, and I will move the world."* —Archimedes

**Figure 2-16.** *Three fulcra of large websites*

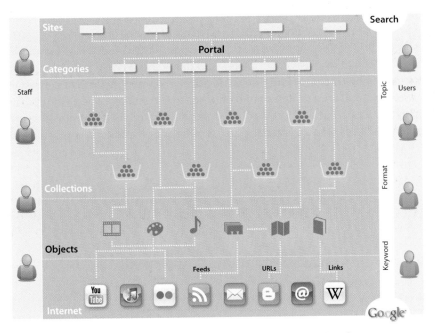

Small Object icons: Created by Joseph Wain and shared under a Creative Commons Attribution license.

**Figure 2-17.** *A concept map*

## PORTAL

The portal, which includes the home page and the top few layers of the website, often presents an opportunity to improve the user experience and the brand. A user-centered redesign that helps people learn about the organization and its services, fosters exploration and discovery, and supports fast, effective search and navigation can make a big impact. Emphasis should be placed on providing multiple paths to the same information so that users can search or browse by format, topic, and keyword. Audience gateways should be provided but not relied upon, since most goal-oriented users won't use them, it's impossible to predict what every member of each audience might want to find, and information-seeking behavior tends to vary more by search expertise and institutional familiarity than by role or profession. The portal should support directed search while enabling discovery. For instance, a robust version of Most Popular (similar to the approach taken by the *New York Times*) can often attract a great deal of interest. In reimagining the portal, it's also worth reconsidering the umbrella architecture, which may include multiple sites, domains, and identities. Are these divisions really useful to users, or do they exist solely as symptoms of organizational dysfunction?

The portal, in conjunction with a content management system, can also serve as a powerful tool for aligning staff efforts and incentives with user needs and goals. First, by establishing design patterns built upon industry best practices, the portal can provide staff in each unit with the tools, templates, and style guides necessary to implement a more consistent identity and suite of interfaces throughout the sites, collections, and documents. Second, since the portal has a significant influence on findability, a clear set of design standards and recommendations has a good chance of adoption. For instance, items should only be directly linked to from the portal if they meet a high standard (e.g., full compliance with the design template), and items should only appear at the top of search results if they meet a middle standard (e.g., assignment of descriptive metadata). The power of findability as a lever can be further strengthened by regular reporting of web analytics. A one-page report that highlights key metrics each month and is widely distributed can improve accountability and sensitivity to user needs and behaviors.

# SEARCH

Massive scale means that search must be positioned at the center of the digital architecture. The portal presents an opportunity to implement a consistent experience through the top layers. However, in the absence of a paradigm shift in our big organization's approach to the Web, it is unrealistic to expect total conformity throughout the site, especially when you consider the inevitable change of technologies and priorities over time. The fact is that browsing simply doesn't scale. At a certain point, it becomes impossible to avoid creating a digital version of the Winchester Mystery House.

And yet, sites and services as diverse as Amazon, Google, Flickr, and Wikipedia have all developed solutions that work despite their lack of centralized control over content and metadata. They have succeeded by embracing search-centered solutions that recognize that searching and browsing must be used in combination to help people effectively navigate. These solutions typically possess the following three qualities:

*Federated*

> Since most users don't know where to look, the site should allow people to perform searches across all of its content. This should not preclude advanced, focused queries on particular collections or databases.

*Faceted*

> The site should embrace faceted navigation (with flexible search scopes) as widely as possible so that users can move fluidly from searching the site to searching a content collection or a product catalog without having to start over or learn a new interface. Global facets might include topic, format, date, and author. Each database might present additional category-specific facets to support narrowing and filtering.

*Fast*

> The organization must invest in the hardware, software, and staff necessary to deliver subsecond response times. Speed is absolutely critical in allowing users to fully engage in an iterative, interactive search experience.

Amazon serves as an excellent example. The site provides fast, federated search across many collections (e.g., books, electronics, toys, and automotive tools). Users can select a category and then search or they can search first, then select a category. Faceted navigation presents users with a customized, interactive map of their results and ample opportunities to narrow or filter those results. Plus, the facets adapt; they progressively conform to the content as users shift between categories or drill down within collections.

**Figure 2-18.** *Amazon's adaptive facets*

Finally, Amazon's Product Pages are easily findable via Google. They have relatively simple URLs to support sharing and inbound links. They also offer options for tagging, rating, and reviewing that ultimately support even better navigation (from the page) and findability (to the page). In short, Amazon's Product Pages are findable, social objects.

## OBJECTS

Similarly, our big organization has an opportunity to make its content more social (viral) and findable by adopting best practices in search engine optimization and social media design. This requires redesigning the objects of search to serve as destinations, gateways, and subjects of conversation. Amazon does this well. So does Flickr. Photos are easily findable via Google or Flickr's own search system, and each photo offers many options for finding similar photos or for finding other photos from the same source, set, pool, or collection. Plus, users are invited to add tags, notes, and comments. Each photo is a catalyst for conversation and community. Additionally, the object isn't stuck on the page. Users can share photos across multiple devices, channels, and services. We can order prints or add our image to stickers, calendars, business cards, T-shirts, magnets, puzzles, and mugs.

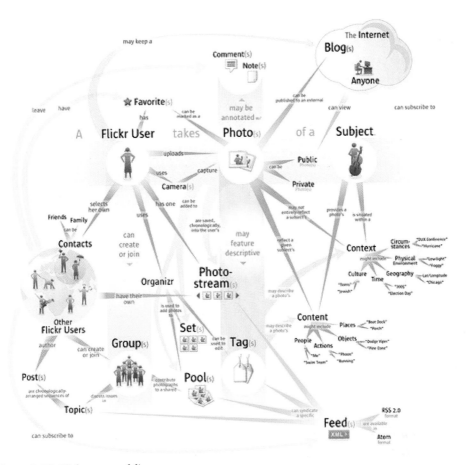

Figure 2-19. *Flickr user model*[4]

This versatility didn't arise by accident. Flickr's About page describes an explicit experience strategy with two main goals:

" *We want to help people make their content available to the people who matter to
them.*

*We want to enable new ways of organizing photos and video.* "

Flickr describes itself as "the WD-40 that makes it easy to get photos or video from one
person to another in whatever way they want" and lists the Web, mobile devices, software applications, RSS feeds, email messages, and blogs as just some of those ways to
import and export content. Finally, Flickr notes that part of the solution is to make the
process collaborative:

---

4 Image by Bryce Glass, *http://soldierant.net/archives/uploads/2007/10/FlickrUserModel_v3.pdf.*

> " *In Flickr, you can give your friends, family, and other contacts permission to organize your stuff—not just to add comments, but also notes and tags. People like to ooh and ahh, laugh and cry, make wisecracks when sharing photos and videos. Why not give them the ability to do this when they look at them over the internet? And as all this info accretes as metadata, you can find things so much easier later on, since all this info is also searchable.* "

In this way, the social and findable elements form a virtuous circle in which conversation promotes findability and vice versa, which is why Flickr has succeeded so well.

## ALL TOGETHER NOW

In conclusion, having identified the objects plus the portal and search as strategic opportunities where leverage affords impact, the trick is weaving them together so that each element becomes a vital part of the whole. This returns us to Amazon, which serves as a great example of a service that has embraced and integrated all three fulcra. The portal supports multiple paths to the same information. It offers federated, faceted, fast search. And it's all built upon an object-oriented foundation that positions Product Pages as the ultimate destination and conversation objects, and as gateways to related content.

Amazon also manages to keep alive the entrepreneurial spirit by engaging the whole ecosystem. With the Kindle, Amazon developed a software and hardware platform for reading e-books and other digital media. With its self-publishing program, Amazon invented a new mix of tools, processes, and incentives to turn users into creators. And, with customer reviews and transparent analytics (e.g., customers who bought this item also bought these items, dynamic sales rank by category), Amazon has made it easier to find and learn. These folks are reinventing publishing by changing the means of production and distribution. They're also designing the ultimate place to search.

By working hard to serve users, refine the interface, tune the engine, enhance the content, and motivate creators while simultaneously striving to leverage and transform the wider context, Amazon and a handful of other pioneering firms are showing us how to make search better. We can't copy all that they do; some solutions are uniquely situated. But we can learn a lot from their example. It's about time we read the writing on the wall.

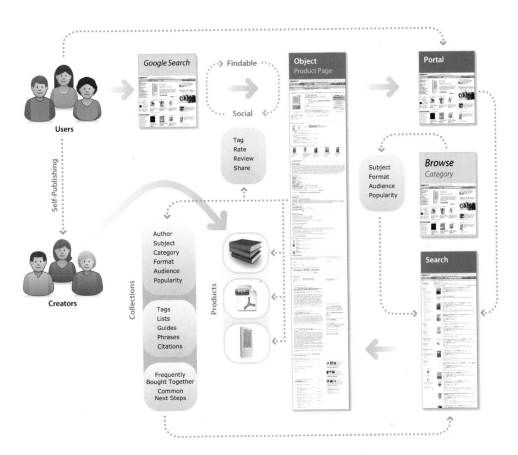

Figure 2-20. *A map of Amazon*

**Figure 2-21.** *The hole in the whole*

In particular, we must improve our ability to zoom in and out. It's essential that we study the anatomy of search. To get each element right requires obsessive attention to detail. We must divide to understand. But we must also dare to lose focus. We must step back and consider the context. Search is only a subset of an information architecture and a wider communication ecology that together shape the user experience.

To make search better, we must ask larger questions. How do we turn users into creators? What are the ingredients for self-organization? Can we achieve our goals without search? How might search inspire us to reach for new goals? To see the big picture, we must know the parts and the whole. We need frameworks, maps, and blueprints; boxes and arrows that help us visualize relationships between a means and the end. But we can't stop with strategy and structure, because search is a system that flows. The interface is only half of interaction. To achieve a holistic understanding of search, we must witness the system and the user in the act, together as one. And for that, we must study behavior.

# Behavior

In music, *improvisation* is the art of creating a song while performing it, in the moment and in response to interplay and interaction. Along with blue notes, polyrhythms, and syncopation, improv is fundamental to the nature of jazz. The freedom and spontaneity of the solo passes from saxophone to piano to trumpet in the call-and-response pattern of African-American field hollers, while the drums and double bass weave a musical fabric in conversational rhythm. Good jazz engages the listener. It's hard to resist the spellbinding power of a player with chops who's in the pocket. We become fully immersed in a state of flow that dissolves the lines between act and actor. As the artist Henri Matisse once noted, "There are wonderful things in real jazz, the talent for improvisation, the liveliness, the being at one with the audience."

In designing the interaction of search, we'd do well to keep jazz in mind, because behavior is a conversation and flow is a state worth striving for. When we search, our actions are reactions to the stimuli of information and interface. The box and its controls shape how we search, and what we find changes what we seek. The distinction between user and system dissolves in behavior. It's an activity that's open to flow. At its best, search absorbs our attention totally. Our experience of time and self are altered. We become lost in the most positive of senses. But we don't get in the groove by accident. As Mihaly Csikszentmihalyi explains, activities such as music, dancing, sailing, and chess are conducive to flow because "they were *designed* to make optimal experience easier to achieve."[1] They offer challenge, give control, support learning, reward skill, and provide feedback. We can both design for flow and experience flow in design, since our practice offers ample challenge and reward for those with the chops to put the swing in search.

---

1 *Flow: The Psychology of Optimal Experience*, Mihaly Csikszentmihalyi (Harper).

**Figure 3-1.** *Behavior is a conversation*

Of course, music isn't written on a blank slate. In the words of Wynton Marsalis, "Improvisation isn't a matter of just making any ol' thing up. Jazz, like any language, has its own grammer and vocabulary. There's no right or wrong, just some choices that are better than others." Similarly, there are patterns of behavior, elements of interaction, and principles of design that form the building blocks of search. The elements are always in flux. Technology shifts interaction from mouse and keyboard to multitouch to freeform gestures in thin air. But our patterns and principles? They're timeless, both limited and inspired by the nature of information and the inherent affordances of our senses.

## PATTERNS OF BEHAVIOR

Search ends with an exit. Users always quit. The question is, why? Did they find what they need or simply give up? Was it the information or the interface? Too little, too much, too slow? Quit is a pattern that demands analytics. We must know the reason they're leaving.

*Quit*

**Figure 3-2.** *Quit is the most common pattern*

For instance, are we sending users away with No Results? If so, perhaps we can improve the interface. In Figure 3-3, Yale University fails to state the system status clearly (e.g., "No results were found"), but otherwise provides a good combination of feedback and next steps. Links to popular pages and popular searches might also be helpful.

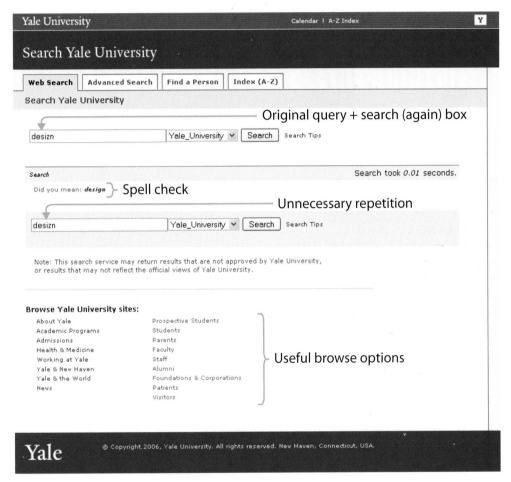

Figure 3-3. *No results at Yale*

On the other hand, if we can help users avoid "No Results" in the first place, that's even better. As Figure 3-4 shows, we're less likely to reach a dead end at Amazon, thanks to the autoexpand strategy of partial match, in which unrecognized keywords are omitted from the query string. Even a match against some search terms may be better than none.

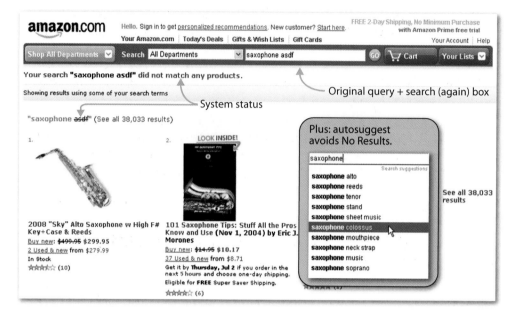

Figure 3-4. *Amazon works to avoid no results*

When users don't quit, they refine. Narrow is the second most common pattern around. Our initial query casts a wide net. Upon seeing results, we pull back. Sometimes, we can avoid such initial imprecision. A wider box invites more words. So does experience with large (and growing) bodies of content. In fact, the average number of keywords per query in web search has moved from 1–2 to 2–3 in recent years.

*Narrow*

Figure 3-5. *Query refinement*

But presearch has its limits. Advance query specification is difficult, because we don't know the size or structure of the index. When we're searching without a map, even a traditional SERP tells us a lot. The nature of snippets and the number of results lets us judge how (and how much) to narrow. In particular, diversity algorithms ensure we can sort out synonyms. Upon seeing sample results from each distinct meaning (e.g., *psychology* versus *cover* flow), we can disambiguate our query.

Even better, faceted navigation puts metadata on the map. As Figure 3-6 shows, Artist Rising lets us clarify whether we want drinking bars (places) or lemon bars (cuisine) and photos or paintings. Plus, we can refine by searching within these results. And even Sort provides a way to limit what we see. Artist Rising offers us many ways to narrow.

Figure 3-6. *Faceted navigation puts metadata on the map*

The opposite pattern is rare. Expand is uncommon, partly because users often cast a wide net to begin, and partly because it's a harder problem. Of course, users can try a broader query. When "low fat lemon bar" returns no results, we omit "low fat" and try again. And we can relax constraints. In Artist Rising, we can undo facet value selections or remove keywords to expand the query by closing the box. We can always take a step back.

*Expand*

**Figure 3-7.** *Casting the net wider*

However, explicit support for expand is rare. It's most commonly seen in the thesaurus browsers of library databases, as shown in Figure 3-8, where structured vocabularies and the risky expectation of searcher expertise afford designers a sense of freedom to reveal the hierarchy (and potential polyhierarchy) that connects to broader terms.

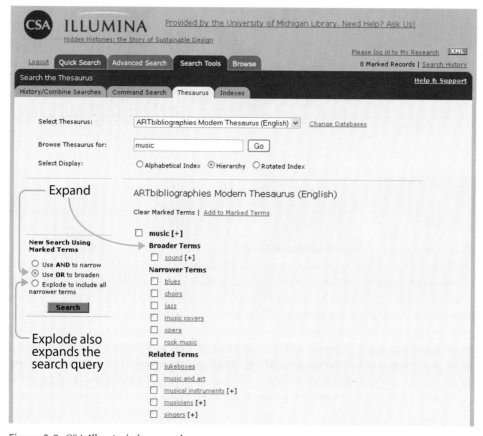

**Figure 3-8.** *CSA Illumina's thesaurus browser*

Rather than a formal hierarchy, search applications often let users expand (or at least explore) by showing related terms within matching categories, as shown in Figure 3-9.

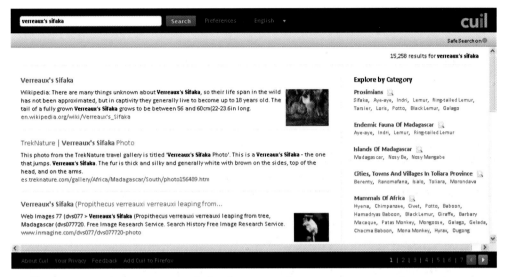

Figure 3-9. *Matching categories and related terms*

Independent of interface, expert searchers employ a singular strategy for expansion known as *pearl growing*. Find one good document, then mine its content and metadata for query terms and leads. We might look for more articles about this topic, by this author, or from this source. Pearl growing is an old trick that's taught in library school.

*Pearl Growing*

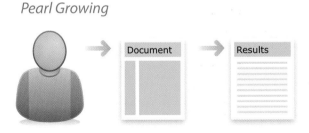

Figure 3-10. *A strategy for finding similar results*

Fortunately, pearl growing is also a strategy we can spread by embedding it within the interface. Google's Similar link is the most ubiquitous example. Although the algorithms may be complex, the user needs only to click a link.

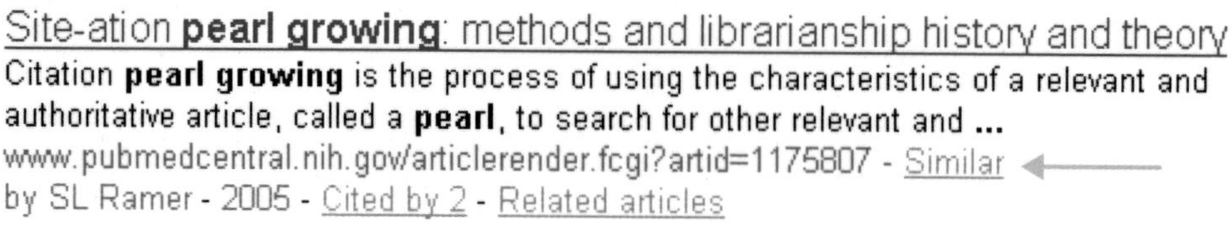

Figure 3-11. *Find similar*

Similarly, music recommender systems make it easy to find songs we like by comparing the attributes, ratings, and collaborative filtering data of songs we know and those we don't. Last.fm and Pandora rely heavily on up and down ratings of individual songs.

Figure 3-12. *Similar controls at Last.fm and Pandora*

iTunes Genius, shown in Figure 3-13, pays more attention to the songs in our personal collections. Either way, these systems make pearl growing fun and easy. From one song, we can find many similar songs to buy and enjoy.

Figure 3-13. *Apple's Genius*

The patterns of behavior we've covered so far—quit, narrow, expand, and pearl grow—are timeless. They are inherent to search. Other patterns (or *antipatterns*) are produced by bad design. For instance, repetitive bouncing between the SERP and individual results is known as *pogosticking*. A little pogosticking means users are sampling results. That's to be expected, but when it happens a lot, it's not sampling; it's a symptom.

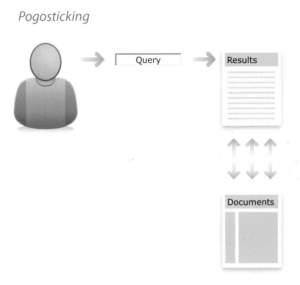

Figure 3-14. *Pogosticking is an antipattern*

Perhaps our snippets and metadata lack the scent users need to effectively scan results, so they must visit each one in turn. Or, if sequential viewing of results is a desirable pattern, we need solutions that support this behavior. Cooliris, shown in Figure 3-15, uses the iPhone's touchscreen to let users flick through image results in linear fashion.

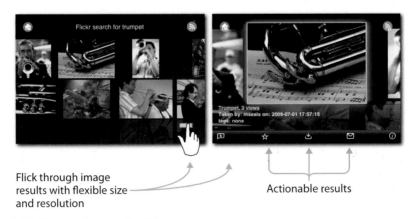

Figure 3-15. *No pogosticking at Cooliris*

Lands' End, shown in Figure 3-16, ensures the metadata and features that users need are available in the gallery of search results. It doesn't stuff too many results on the page at the expense of rich summaries. A clear product image, displaying the sole on rollover, inline color selection, the name, and the price are just the right mix for most users.

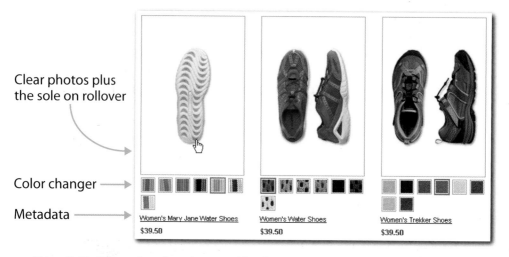

Clear photos plus the sole on rollover

Color changer

Metadata

Figure 3-16. *Gallery of search results at Lands' End*

Another common antipattern is *thrashing*. In thrashing, a design flaw resides in users' heads in the form of the anchoring bias. We set the anchor with our initial query, and then, despite poor results, we insist on small variations of the flawed search phrase rather than trying new approaches.

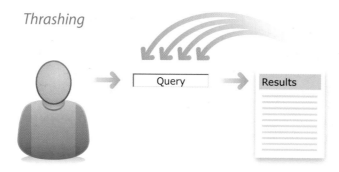

*Thrashing*

Figure 3-17. *Thrashing derives from the anchoring bias*

For instance, a user searching for a concert may try many queries that begin with the (misspelled) nickname rather than switching to the performer's full name.

*sachmo*
*sachmo concert*
*sachmo jazz concert*
*sachmo jazz festival*
*sachmo music festival*
*sachmo summer celebration*

In Figure 3-18, Yahoo! illustrates two ways to break this pattern. First, autocomplete helps users avoid typos and get the query right to begin with. Second, autosuggest can recommend related queries that don't include the original search term. This feature taps query reformulation data, the terms users enter after their first search fails, to make this semantic leap and help users who start in the wrong place to weigh anchor and move on.

Figure 3-18. *Autocomplete and autosuggest at Yahoo!*

In fact, by identifying related concepts, autosuggest helps users to move forward (refine), backward (expand), and sideways (related). Like many good design patterns, autosuggest multitasks. It's a timely solution to a timeless problem. After all, both autocomplete and autosuggest are recent additions online, made possible by the advance of technology. Even as core patterns of behavior endure, design patterns must adjust to new possibilities, which is why we must keep our eyes (and ears) attuned to the elements of interaction.

# ELEMENTS OF INTERACTION

It's a stimulating period for the practice of interaction design. Emerging technologies reinvent what's possible, new platforms challenge old metaphors, sensors add extra senses, and all this innovation disrupts our cozy patterns. A rare burst of evolutionary change is reshaping our expectations of interface. While the desktop still reigns supreme, the rapid adoption and improvement of mobile devices has our attention. The sensors and actuators of multitouch and gestural interaction are on our minds. Rich user interfaces blur the boundaries of web, desktop, and mobile applications. Design patterns flow back and forth between platforms in strange loops that keep us all on our toes. At such a heady time, it's worth reviewing the elements of interaction that bind us to each platform.

The desktop is the most established platform and the main gateway to search. We all know the standard configuration: mouse, keyboard, monitor, speakers, and sometimes a video camera and microphone for audiovisual input. Once in a while we Ctrl-C a trick from the old command-line interface (CLI), but mostly we click and double-click the graphical user interface (GUI), dragging and dropping files and folders as we go. It's a short distance from desktop to web, where sites and pages with URLs are simply new places for old faces. The boundaries are barely worth mention. Rollovers, hovers, clicks, and keywords are the main events, while menus, buttons, form fields, and links are the basic interface idioms.

In search, rich elements include scented widgets, Ajaxian calendars, DHTML sliders, radial menus, dynamic transitions, transparent overlays, drag-and-drop results, and advanced query wizards. There's a great deal of freedom, and that's part of the problem. In the absence of solid design process and principles, these rich elements give us more rope with which to hang our users. All too often, we sacrifice usability and accessibility for a sexy look and feel. Finding the right balance isn't easy, mind you. The wealth of our palette affords us the paradox of choice, and we're still learning to design the results.

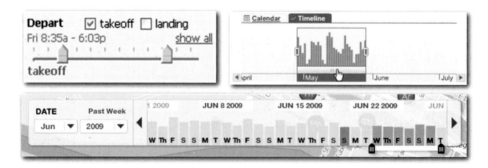

Figure 3-19. *Sliders for filtering results*

Of course, we can't dwell on the desktop. Mobile is the fastest growing platform ever, and for many designers it's the most interesting to boot. While it may add tiny screens and keyboards to our constraints, mobile also creates fabulous new avenues for inter-action. Multitouch lets us tap to open, spread to zoom, and slide to scroll. A camera, microphone, and speakers offer multisensory I/O, and our devices know where they go. Location, altitude, bearing, and velocity are all new inputs for queries we have yet to conceive. Plus, the accelerometer lets us rotate to landscape, shake to clear, and lift to search. Sensors and actuators presage an era of gestural interaction beyond the device.

Figure 3-20. *Mobile search interaction*

While the Clapper is old and the Wii is popular, freeform gestural interaction is still in its infancy. Our presence opens doors, our hands turn on taps, and for paper towels, we wave to activate. However, our gestural vocabulary is limited and rarely applied to search. That said, it's not too early to begin imagining gestural query interfaces and idioms for freeform discovery. In fact, now is precisely the time to think about how we want to search, before the next wave of innovation hype masks our view with froth and frivolity.

It's smart to start with our senses. We can see, hear, touch, smell, and taste. We can sense acceleration, balance, pain, and the relative position of our body parts. We can feel a haptic buzz. How might we tap these channels of input and output? We can already search by singing. What's next? Of course, we shouldn't stop with our senses, since our sensors can know so much more. Location is just the beginning. Sensors can detect and measure everything from magnetic fields and air pollution around the globe to the heart rate and glucose levels of a single human body. Already, as shown in Figure 3-21, Ambient Devices is turning everyday objects into wireless information appliances. The umbrella's handle pulses when rain is forecast, and the orb glows different colors to display real-time stock market trends, traffic patterns, pollen forecasts, and more. Sensors are enabling us to search beyond our senses, and together with new devices and rich interfaces, they're transforming the how, what, where, when, and why of discovery.

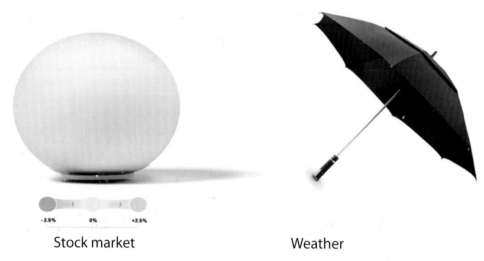

Stock market                                    Weather

**Figure 3-21.** *Information at a glance from Ambient Devices*

We are also searching across channels. For many applications, we can't limit or predict the context of use. The experience is out of control. A search may start at home on the desktop, move to mobile on the bus, continue on an in-store kiosk, and end in the shelves. And it may have been a television or radio advertisement or a highway bill-board that provoked the search in the first place.

That's why smart organizations take the time to map touchpoints across media and channels. By employing user experience research and service design principles to iden-tify, optimize, and align all important interfaces and interactions with their products, services, and brands, organizations are able to improve customer satisfaction and the bottom line. Apple is the most famous case. The distinct features and the relationships between the iPod in your palm, the iTunes desktop application, and the iTunes Store on the Web serve as a familiar model. Apple's genius was to locate key functions on the right platforms. As shown in Figure 3-22, we play on the device, manage on the desktop, and buy at the store. Of course, we search across all three. Early iPods and iPhones lacked search. It wasn't necessary until it was. Now, it's both a feature and a multichannel oppor-tunity, because Apple needs better design and integration across platforms. The search applications are there, at last. But they're not insanely great!

Figure 3-22. *Apple's many interfaces*

There are many less well-known examples. For instance, the Ann Arbor Library supports a successful cross-channel search experience. A catalog query on a desktop or mobile device offers "Request this title" for each result. Patrons can have books and other items shipped to their local branches, and receive email alerts when those items arrive. Patrons can arrange for pickup at the reserve shelf or from a convenient after-hours locker, and when an item gets many requests, the library buys more copies—there's a feedback loop that improves results.

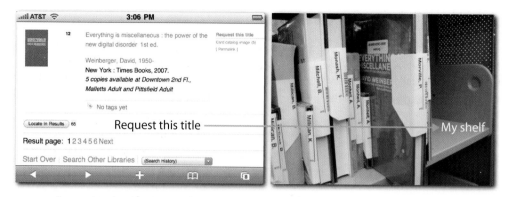

Figure 3-23. *Cross-channel design at the Ann Arbor District Library*

And then there are those things that make us think. For instance, as shown in Figure 3-24, WineM is a "smart" wine rack made by ThingM that uses radio frequency identification (RFID) to track individual bottles in a rack. A mobile device lets users query the collection by year, region, type, and price. Full-color LED lights transform the rack and bottles into a physical faceted search results interface.

Figure 3-24. *WineM's faceted search interface*

In search interaction, the genie is out of the bottle. When we can do so much in and out of the box, there's no going back. But we may come to pine for old limits. While the freedom to invent idioms and change channels makes design more interesting, it also makes our work more difficult. It's all too easy to create elaborate, confusing interfaces that make our users come unglued. That's why we must stick to our principles.

# PRINCIPLES OF DESIGN

Humans began using pigments such as ochres and iron oxides for colorful body decoration around 400,000 BCE. It took us a bit longer to invent written language (about 5,500 years ago). Since then, we've been creating and combining images, symbols, and words to communicate ideas and meaning. We've had time to practice design.

Of course, time is the last thing we have when users visit a search interface. In the first 250 milliseconds, the preattentive variables of size, shape, position, alignment, orientation, color, and texture have already worked their magic. A well-crafted interface reveals its core features and layout to our subconscious before we have time to think.

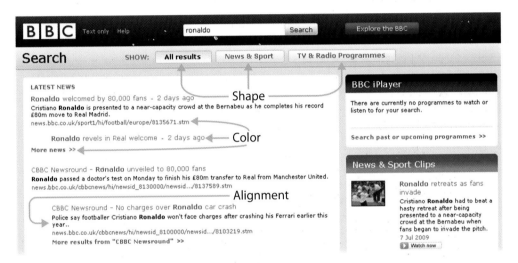

*Figure 3-25. Preattentive variables at the BBC*

This magic doesn't occur naturally. Great interfaces require talented designers who know how to use visual hierarchy to organize information and guide action, and who appreciate the importance of detail. For instance, early versions of Google's spellcheck stated, "If you didn't find what you were looking for…" at the top of the page, along with the suggested spelling. Nobody noticed it, so Google tested shorter variations such as, "Did you mean:" above and below the results—and use increased dramatically.

Designers must also be sensitive to context. In music, for instance, the animated 3D interface of Cover Flow makes sense. It's fun to flip through colorful covers while listening to and searching for our favorite songs and albums. But this sexy design enjoys limited play in other categories. It certainly doesn't belong in web search, where simplicity and speed are so vital. As Google's user experience director, Irene Au, explains:

> " *A lot of designers want to increase the line height or padding in order to make the interface 'breathe.' We deliberately don't do that. We want to squeeze in as much information as possible above the fold. We recognize that information density is part of what makes the experience great and efficient. Our goal is to get users in and out really quickly. All our design decisions are based on that strategy.* " 2

This statement reveals an important dimension of design. We can't be concerned solely with how an interface looks. As Steve Jobs famously remarked, "Design is how it works." Visual design shapes the first impression and has a lasting impact, but the halo effect carries the tune only so far. Interaction design is the missing link that lets the rough edges between user and system dissolve in behavior. It's a discipline essential to flow. And it's a practice that's relatively new—although we've made tools for over a million years, we've been making interactive software for less than a century. That said, we've made a good start at defining first principles, and many of them apply directly to search.

## INCREMENTAL CONSTRUCTION

We can accomplish amazing feats once we overcome fear and inertia at the start line. But oftentimes we don't start. We're overwhelmed by the enormity of a task or confused by the complexity of an interface. These feelings are so widespread that we collect idioms for inspiration. Get the ball rolling. Rome wasn't built in a day. A journey of a thousand miles begins with a single step. Don't make me think! Designers should heed these words, because search is a terribly common place to stop. A complex interface hits like a brick wall. Not only does it make users think, but it also makes them feel stupid, and that's the kiss of death. So, we must recall the paradox of the active user and allow users to start small, with a keyword or two. Input hints or prompts near or within the box should show the what and the how of search, and the box should boast autocomplete and a forgiving format. Why should users worry about spelling and syntax when that's our job?

Let's get them started with good defaults and keep them moving with facets, filters, and intriguing branches. We must also support safe exploration by enabling undo, so users can modify parameters, step back, or start over. We must work hard to lower search costs and reduce barriers to entry, because search isn't iterative and interactive when users stop before they begin. People will build great queries incrementally, one click at a time, if we can get them past the start line and always offer at least one next step.

---

2 "Google's Irene Au: On Design Challenges," *Business Week* (March 18, 2009), *www.businessweek.com/innovate/content/mar2009/id20090318_786470.htm.*

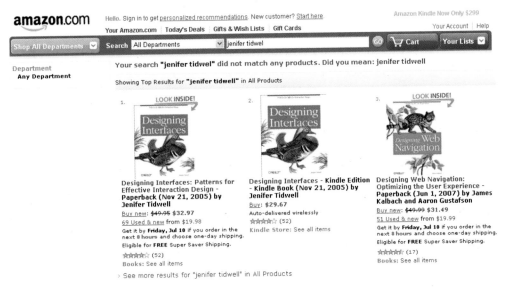

Figure 3-26. *Forgiving format at Amazon*

## PROGRESSIVE DISCLOSURE

Experience with a tool or task often shifts the optimal balance of power and simplicity. To begin, users don't want to be overwhelmed with features. But with time, more advanced options may be desirable. So, progressive disclosure defers these powerful or specialized features to a secondary screen, making software easier to use and learn. We must design applications that require the least amount of physical and mental effort, using contextual tools like hover-reveal to offer an invitation without cluttering the interface.

Google Maps offers a good example of progressive disclosure and careful adherence to the user dictate: "Show me only what I want." The initial interface is a basic map with an overlay for popular tasks like getting directions. A click adds a colorful traffic layer and a hover reveals more options. Google designs disclosures that are responsive to users.

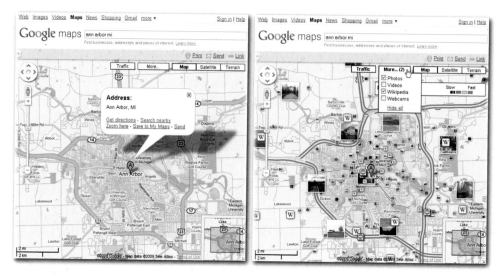

Figure 3-27. *Progressive disclosure in Google Maps*

Faceted navigation is a similarly progressive design pattern. Users can begin with a few keywords and end with a few results. They can ignore the facets if they choose, but the power of incremental query refinement is available, plus the quantity and specificity of metadata fields often snowballs helpfully as they go. Facets allow people to learn search on gentle slopes rather than being forced into the big step from the bunny hills of the basic interface to the black diamond mode of advanced search.

In general, even though progressive disclosure may suggest the use of modes to prevent specialized features from cluttering the basic interface, we must take great care when introducing distinct system states like advanced search. Modes often lead to mode errors in which users forget the current state, attempt an action belonging in another mode, and get an unexpected result. These are not insurmountable problems, but it's often easiest for everyone to rally around a modeless interface. Similarly, it's best to add flexibility with support for deferred choices. Let the user search and then log in without losing results. Offering many paths to the same destination effectively supports both incremental construction and progressive disclosure. We get two principles for the price of one.

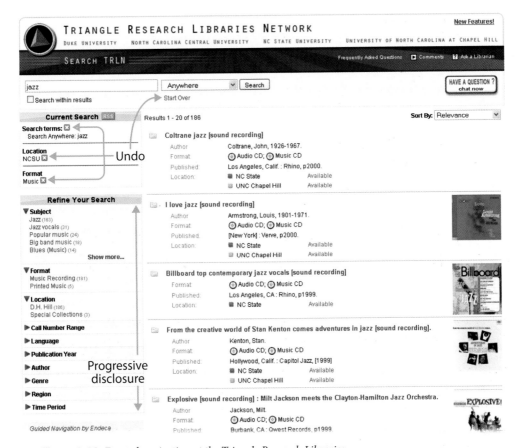

Figure 3-28. *Faceted navigation at the Triangle Research Libraries*

## IMMEDIATE RESPONSE

Poor performance will turn any interface into a train wreck. Flow requires feedback, early and often. A few years ago, results were the only reply. Our goal was a subsecond response. Now, with autocomplete and autosuggest, the results may precede the query. How's that for timely feedback? Of course, our systems can't always deliver, in which case we rely on animations, cinematic effects, and other visual transitions to indicate progress and enhance engagement. But while transitions advance the perception of performance, they're no substitute for speed, which can improve even a mediocre system by enabling iterative, interactive query refinement in response to results.

Volkswagen UK employs a wonderfully subtle form of feedback. During active control of a slider, the options to be excluded from the results fade to gray. Then, upon release of the mouse button, the faded options disappear, and the remaining cars gracefully shift into position within the smaller result set. It takes a while for this rich Internet application to load, but once running, it's a smooth ride with great performance and quick response.

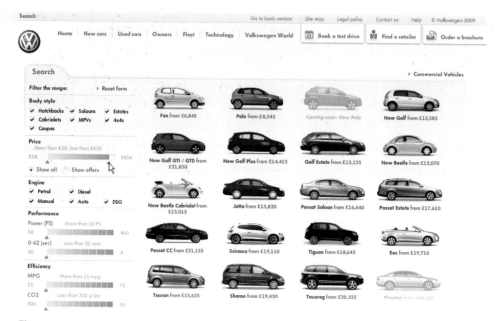

Figure 3-29. *Immediate response at Volkswagen UK*

## ALTERNATE VIEWS

For many applications, the optimal view differs by user and task. One size does not fit all. This is certainly true in search, where the ideal mix of metadata depends upon user intent. A linear list of results rendered in text may work for quick lookup, but comparison shopping merits a tabular presentation with images. Conversely, the search for co-occurrence invites a geographic map with symbolic data overlays. Since we can't always employ the query to accurately interpret intent, it's important to provide the user with choices.

Viewzi takes alternate views to the extreme. This intriguing application provides the basic choice between small and large images, but it doesn't stop there. Viewzi offers more than 18 different ways to view search results. Options include simple text, image grid, timeline, tag cloud, and a fashionable cover flow interface for browsing web screen-shots. It's not a model that most should emulate, but it does get us thinking about the layouts and lenses we might offer our users.

Figure 3-30. *Multiple views with Viewzi*

Sort order also provides users with the choice of alternate views. Since users rarely explore beyond the first page of results, sorts act much like filters. When we sort by most popular or best rated, we effectively limit our view by that criteria. On the other hand, we sometimes sort by date or title so we can quickly scan the list for a known item. Sort order is a relatively easy way to provide users with flexibility and control.

Figure 3-31. *Controls for sort order*

Another alternate view worth reflection is that of those who can't see. As with other features of an application, search should be universally accessible. Clearly, this means that search and result interfaces must be easy to navigate with text-to-speech and Braille output screen readers. It's also worth considering the content. Google's Accessible Search, for instance, relies upon signals in HTML markup to identify and prioritize search results that are easier for blind and visually impaired users to use. As designers, we must make content and functionality accessible by adhering to the layered strategy of progressive enhancement (or the inverse principle of graceful degradation). It's our responsibility to offer multiple paths to the same information to provide all users with freedom and to serve those who lack the basic options many of us take for granted.

## PREDICTABILITY

For most applications, predictability assures usability. Effectiveness, efficiency, and satisfaction generally follow when users can accurately predict what will happen next. In search, we need predictable features and results. Controls must be easy to discover and understand. The Gap, for instance, uses a simple hover invitation to feed-forward the Quick Look feature, which leads to an overlay instead of the detailed product page. Since the invite appears in the natural flow of result selection, it's impossible to miss.

Figure 3-32. *Hover invitation at The Gap*

In contrast, Bloomberg's rotate-to-view feature is less discoverable, but once found it works well, because it's simple and consistent. When a gesture works the same way throughout an application, habituation improves efficiency. Users become comfortable with that gesture and know what to expect.

Figure 3-33. *Rotate to view at Bloomberg*

Consistency of placement is also important. When people use controls, they find and recognize them by location. So, in designing search and result interfaces, we must respect the power of spatial memory and position controls and widgets consistently.

Of course, search only works well when results are predictable. First, the box must do what's expected by responding with the right results in good order. Second, each result must offer sufficient scent through the right mix of metadata so that users can sense its aboutness. We can't have people wondering what's hidden behind door number one.

## RECOGNITION OVER RECALL

Recognition is triggered by context. We're quite good at it. With the radio on, we can sing the lyrics to thousands of songs. Recall works without context. At this, we're terribly bad. With the radio off, our memories fade to black. This imbalance is shared across our senses, and it's a huge factor in design. It's a major reason why we shifted from CLI to GUI. Users couldn't recall commands, but they could easily recognize buttons and links.

In search, the first step is to make valuable options visible. Otherwise, users forget what they can do. This requires compromise with progressive disclosure. We need just the right balance between show and hide. Second, we must offer tools that reduce users' short-term memory load. Amazon is the best in this department. While searching, users can use a shopping cart, shopping list, and wish list as their personal memory managers.

But Amazon further boosts our memories by thinking outside the box. Users can drag the universal wish list button to their browsers' toolbars, and then add items to wish lists while exploring any online store. Even better, while out and about in the physical world, users can tap the Remembers feature of Amazon's mobile application to snap photos of anything they wish to remember. If the object is a product, Amazon will try to find it and send an email alert with a link, then show it on the home page the next time the user visits. It's a truly amazing feature that makes it almost impossible to forget what we intended to buy.

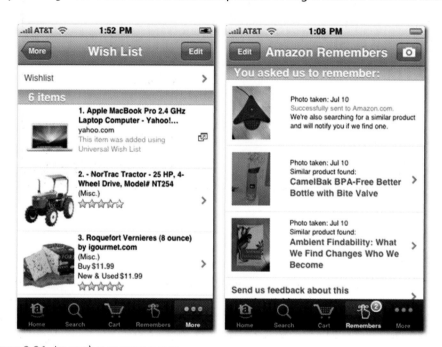

**Figure 3-34.** *Amazon's memory managers*

Of course, sometimes the path to better recognition in search is browse. Search requires that we know what we want and have the words to describe our needs. In contrast, browse illustrates what's available, shows the vocabulary, and reminds us of things we might need.

In mobile, browse is especially useful, because it takes time to type and we're unsure what to search for. Applications like Where and AroundMe don't require users to remember the types of things to be found. Instead, we can browse the map or a traditional taxonomy. We may not recall what we want, but we'll recognize it when we see it.

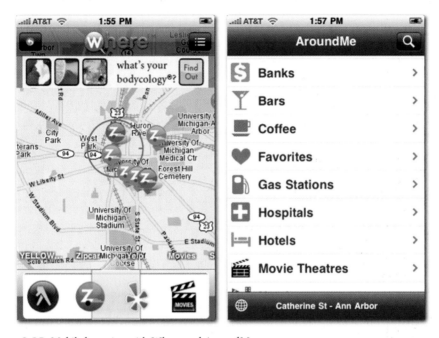

Figure 3-35. *Mobile browsing with Where and AroundMe*

## MINIMAL DISRUPTION

In light of our feeble memories, not to mention our general impatience and intolerance for change, it's often best (when possible) to stay on the page. Modern applications usually offer such conveniences as same page error messages, edit in place, and contextual help. Overlays, inlays, tabs, virtual scrolling and panning, and inline paging are all creative ways to bring additional content and controls into the picture without shifting the frame.

Netflix takes convenience a step further. In addition to a detail overlay, Netflix serves up actionable results, so we can add items to the Instant Queue or start playing a movie, all without leaving the results page. The controls and features move so we don't have to.

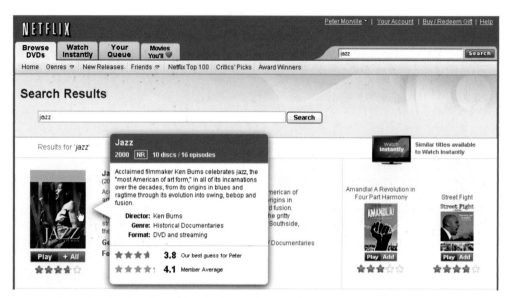

Figure 3-36. *A detail overlay and actionable results at Netflix*

## DIRECT MANIPULATION

Yet another factor in the success of GUI is the principle of direct manipulation. Interfaces that enable users to interact directly with visible objects are more easily learned and used. Sometimes we rely on real-world metaphors. We sort files on the desktop and drag them into the trash can. Other times, our idioms have no analog, yet direct manipulation drives them into our muscle memory. Our bodies remember what our minds forget.

At first blush, search has little room for direct manipulation. After all, isn't the box ground zero for the triumphant rebirth of the command line? But upon reflection, we find opportunities for tangible results. For instance, Searchme lets users drag results into custom search stacks for later review or for sharing with friends and colleagues. There's also an Add to Stack link, but it lacks the visual and tactile gratification of drag-and-drop.

Figure 3-37. *Drag results to stacks at Searchme*

However, the link also lacks the problems of drag-and-drop. The perceived affordance of the link is clear. Predictability is high, and it favors recognition over recall. In contrast, there's no perceived affordance to indicate the results are draggable. Searchme fails to provide a self-describing drag handle. It does a better job with the transition and drop zone. Upon result selection, the stack area lights up and the result spins and shrinks until it's dropped into place. But this introduces another challenge. The use of drag-and-drop invokes Fitts' Law: the time to acquire a target is a function of the distance to and size of the target. This means we must think carefully about the size and placement of the drop zone. Many users have a hard time getting the mouse (and cursor or drag handle) into just the right place, especially while holding down the mouse button.

The pie menu (also known as a radial menu) is an interesting alternative. A music search engine named Songza illustrates the benefits. First, it's self-revealing. When a user clicks on a result, the menu appears. Second, it plays well with Fitts' Law. The options, including those within the nested menus, are near the original point of interaction. Third, it's a gestural interface with the advantages of direct manipulation. Expert users can rely on muscle memory to select options without glancing at menus.

Figure 3-38. *Songza's self-revealing pie menu*

Of course, we must consider how these principles of design interact. For instance, the pursuit of direct manipulation may compromise accessibility, or our basic controls may simply fail the power user. It's a constant balancing act that can only be done in context.

## CONTEXT OF USE

In design, context is a seven-letter word that means everything. It's not enough for our applications to work great in the lab; they must succeed in the real world. This means we must consider users, goals, content, features, platform, and environment. An elderly man with fat fingers may have a hard time using the tiny touch targets of a soft keyboard to search for a nearby restaurant while bouncing on a bus. That's why the iPhone employs iceberg tips and adaptive targets to make writing a little easier. It's also why Google Mobile uses search history, autosuggest, and voice search to let us type a little less.

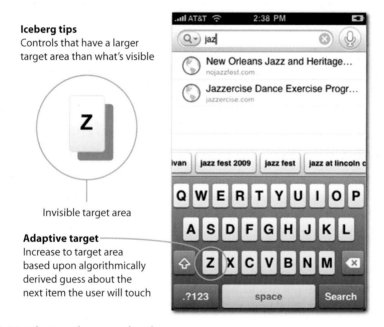

Figure 3-39. *Adaptive solutions on the iPhone*

Of course, we're all making it up as we go along. There's no sheet music for what we do, since each context requires a new song. Interaction elements and design principles afford us a basic grammar and vocabulary. We can even string together a lick here and there by drawing upon established patterns of design. But, at the end of the day, innovation requires improvisation. We won't find flow, get in the groove, or create designs that dissolve in behavior without embracing the risk of new rhythms. As Louis Armstrong once noted, "Never play a thing the same way twice." It's time we put the jazz in design.

# 4

# Design Patterns

" *The design of the garden lies within the language.* "

—Christopher Alexander

A *language* is a system of symbols and rules to convey ideas and information. We rely on natural languages like English, Spanish, and Swahili to communicate with one another. We use artificial languages like SQL, Perl, and Java to specify instructions and behavior. These language types have much in common, but they differ with respect to rules. Artificial languages are planned and constructed by an individual or group. Their vocabularies and syntax are precisely defined. In contrast, natural languages emerge and evolve in unpremeditated fashion. They're spoken before they're written and only later do we derive the rules (like "i" before "e" except after "c"), which are riddled with *weird* exceptions because they're not really rules at all. In fact, "patterns" is a better word. Patterns allow for emergence, evolution, and imperfection. We can detect patterns and adapt them to our needs. They are free of charge and subject to change. And yet, access does not ensure success. Eloquence requires sensitivity to structure and situation. How do our patterns work together within specific contexts? And which patterns are we missing?

These are the tough questions we often ignore. While Christopher Alexander is most famous for his patterns, he's the first to point out their limits. He notes, "The links between the patterns are almost as much a part of the language as the patterns themselves." He argues that how we put the patterns together makes all the difference:

" *The difference between prose and poetry is not that different languages are used, but that the same language is used differently. In an ordinary English sentence, each word has one meaning, and the sentence too, has one simple meaning. In a poem, the meaning is far more dense. Each word carries several meanings; and the sentence as a whole carries an enormous density of interlocking meanings, which together illuminate the whole.* " [1]

Finally, Alexander warns of the dangers of language by invoking the linguistic relativity of the Whorf hypothesis—the idea that language shapes (and constrains) thought. To avoid limiting the solution space, we must give our language sufficient expressive power. Even then, when faced with new problems, we must be ready to change the language or leave it behind. As Alexander concludes, "This ageless character has nothing, in the end, to do with languages. The language, and the processes which stem from it,

---

1 *A Pattern Language*, Christopher Alexander (Oxford University Press).

merely release the fundamental order which is native to us." The timeless way and the quality without a name flow naturally from observing and responding to human behavior within an environmental context. The language is a map, but empathy is the key.

As we study the patterns of search, we'd do well to heed these lessons from disciplines more storied than ours. After all, the design of search is a new and rapidly evolving practice. We're still working on the basic alphabet, even as we aspire to the poetry of language. We design applications that work beautifully, but then struggle to repeat our success. Getting the design right and the right design often feels like trying to catch lightning in a bottle. That's because all too often we don't understand *why* the design works. We search for solutions by trial and error. It's a long, risky process and sometimes there's no alternative, but often there is a better, more timeless way.

In this chapter, we'll survey 10 patterns that have emerged as repeatable solutions to common problems. Simply identifying and describing each pattern has value, but we won't stop there. We'll explore how each pattern relates to others and which contexts are most suitable to which patterns. Most importantly, we'll ask *why*. Why does this pattern work? Why is this a common problem? Why have we selected this solution? In this final question, we sow the seeds of innovation. Can we escape the limits of existing tools and templates? Is there a better way? Answering this question may require modifying the fundamental system of symbols and patterns that we use to communicate our ideas. After all, as the architect said, "The design of the garden lies within the language."

## AUTOCOMPLETE

The autocomplete design pattern is a good place to start. As users type into a text entry box, suggestions appear automatically. It's a pattern that first emerged within the Help functions of desktop applications. This solution solves several very common problems. First, typing takes time. Second, users can't spell well. Third, we're often at a loss for words. We simply don't know or can't remember the right terms. Since these problems are portable, it was only a matter of time before the pattern spread. Autocomplete is now a familiar fixture across desktop, web, and mobile platforms (Figure 4-1).

A major prerequisite of autocomplete is a source of data for suggestions. Classic desktop applications rely on an alphabetical index of help topics. Google draws from a user's personal search history and from the collective search behavior of many users (Figure 4-2). Firefox (also shown in Figure 4-2) taps browsing history and bookmarks. Yahoo! steps beyond autocomplete to autosuggest, shown in Figure 4-3, by tapping query reformulation data to recommend related queries that need not include the original search term.

Figure 4-1. *Autocomplete in a desktop application*

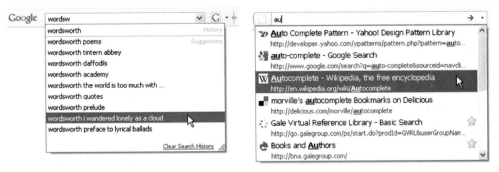

Figure 4-2. *Autocomplete in Google and Firefox*

Figure 4-3. *Autocomplete and autosuggest*

Autosuggest can help users to pivot by highlighting alternate concepts and relevant verticals. It's worth noting that while autocomplete and autosuggest are distinct concepts, most applications blend them together for a small footprint. Consequently, in this book, we've bundled both under the autocomplete pattern.

A pioneer in this area, Yahoo! has also experimented with visual autocomplete, shown in Figure 4-4. Sometimes users are able to clarify better with an image than a word.

Figure 4-4. *Visual autocomplete*

Many websites, such as Apple.com, draw from their product catalogs to suggest Best Bets rather than popular queries, allowing users to skip search and go directly to their destination. Reference sites like Answers.com, shown in Figure 4-5, draw upon a structured database to support query disambiguation, helping users to clarify before they search.

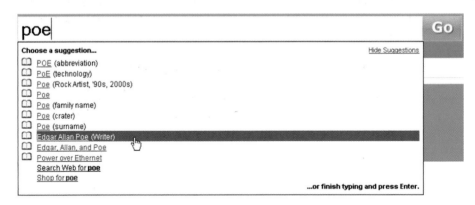

Figure 4-5. *Autocomplete at Answers.com*

On the mobile platform, autocomplete is clearly a natural. Small, shaky keyboards are not conducive to text entry, so Google and Yahoo! work overtime to recall past searches, suggest common queries, and recommend popular destinations, all before we've typed the first word. Of course, autocomplete isn't the only solution to this common problem—both Google and Yahoo! support mobile voice search. We can't limit ourselves to refinement and continuous improvement. We should also strive to innovate with novel approaches and complementary solutions. We must think outside the box.

Figure 4-6. *Autocomplete in Google and Yahoo! Mobile*

For instance, autocomplete isn't only about typing and spelling. Suggestions help us when we're not sure what to seek. On websites, the information architecture provides users with structural and semantic clues that precede and inform the search. Similarly, in mobile applications, we use categories and icons to invite users to explore with a click. In this way, browse complements search by getting folks started and helping them learn what to seek.

Figure 4-7. *Browse options in Citysearch and Dopplr*

In summary, autocomplete is a flexible pattern that works across multiple platforms. And, it's fairly discrete. It can coexist with or function independently of other patterns.

Figure 4-8. *The Autocomplete design pattern*

That said, autocomplete can draw suggestions from a Best Bets database and may leverage algorithms from the best first pattern. Autocomplete can also work well with scoped search and personalized search, since it's easier to make good suggestions when the scope is limited and when we have insight into searcher behavior and intent. However, as Figure 4-9 shows, organizations don't always tune suggestions to a specific category. It's unlikely that "kerosene heater" is a popular query among users looking for books.

Figure 4-9. *Autosuggest with scoped search*

# BEST FIRST

In search, you're only as good as your first results. While the exact numbers vary by system and depend upon the users, the task, and the interface, it's a safe bet that the top three results will draw 80 percent of the attention. The remaining results on the first page may each earn a few percentage points. After that, visibility drops off a cliff.

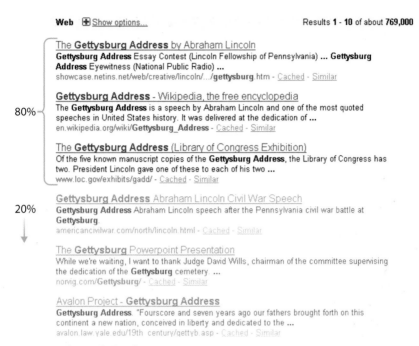

Figure 4-10. *Best first with Google*

This is important for two reasons. First, surfacing great results satisfies the simplest use case for search. Users enter queries, scan the first few results, click a link, and the search is complete. *Best first* is crucial to making search simple, fast, and relevant. Second, the first few results inordinately influence query reformulation. Users enter search terms, scan and learn from the first few results, and try a different query. For the 25–50 percent of search sessions that involve query reformulation, those first three results are a vital part of the user interface. What we find changes what we seek.

Consequently, best first must be a top priority during search engine selection. High-quality, transparent, flexible result-ranking algorithms are critical to success. They must be good out of the gate, and they should support tuning to the unique requirements of a particular content collection or application. The algorithms should account for:

*Relevance*
>   These algorithms focus on topical relevance or aboutness. They aim to match the query keywords to the text of the content and metadata. Effective algorithms account for term order, proximity, location, frequency, and document length. An exact phrase match in a short title is worth more than an AND co-occurrence in a long body. A phrase that repeats on a page but is rare on the site merits extra weight. Relevance algorithms must also manage the transformation of text queries to account for plurals and other word variants (e.g., poet and poetry). Tuning may be required to get the right balance of precision and recall. Relevance is typically the default setting and is often in truth a hybrid that combines the inputs of multiple algorithms into a balanced solution.

*Popularity*

> In most contexts, social data can deliver a big boost to semantic algorithms. Google's PageRank, which counts links as votes, was the first mainstream success. Today, popularity is typically a multialgorithmic measure. At Flickr, a photo's *interestingness* derives from views, comments, notes, bookmarks, favorites, and so on. At Amazon, users can sort by Bestselling or Best Reviews, but even when they sort by relevance, social data influences the results.

*Date*

> Sorting by date is rarely a good default, but it is a useful option, especially for news and email applications in which reverse chronological order (newest first) is relatively common. In many cases, the date of publication or modification can serve as a valuable input into the general-purpose relevance algorithm by improving the freshness of top results.

*Format*

> In pure form, format and content type are most useful as filters, allowing users to view only images, videos, or news. However, they can also help to boost the best results. For instance, on an intranet, HTML and PDF documents may be more polished than *.doc* or *.xls* files. In such cases, application-specific tuning that brings the best formats to the top is extremely valuable.

*Personalization*

> A user's search history, social network, or current location (online or off) are just a few inputs that might influence the order of results. We'll delve into this topic when we explore the personalized search pattern. For now, let's just note that personalization is at least as difficult as it is desirable.

*Diversity*

> In search, it's easy to get too much of a good thing. Diversity algorithms guard against redundant results and support query clarification and refinement by surfacing distinct meanings (e.g., apple and AAPL) and formats. Application-specific tuning delivers the right balance and a nice blend of results.

As designers, we need not understand exactly how these algorithms work, but they must be on our requirements list during search engine selection. We must tune them to our content or application. Generally, a blended default is in order. Users typically want results that are relevant, popular, and timely. A pure sort order, like the one shown in Figure 4-11, is a nice option but a poor default. Since *The Little Prince* is among the most popular books ever written, that's most likely the best first result. But without algorithms enhanced by social data, this library database serves up *The Little Lame Prince* instead.

Figure 4-11. *Sort by title ignores popularity*

Of course, algorithms aren't the only way to the top. While we must rely on software and distributed user behavior (e.g., tagging, bookmarking) to manage the long tail of search, applying centralized editorial effort to suggest Best Bets for the most common queries delivers a substantial return on investment. In most cases, the analysis of search query data reveals a power law distribution and invites us to apply the 80/20 rule. A small number of unique search phrases accounts for a large percentage of total queries. It has become a best practice for managers of large websites to integrate a simple database that matches these common search phrases to good starting points or destinations.

Best Bets goes by many names, including Suggested Links, Recommended Results, and Editor's Choice. Figure 4-13 shows that Microsoft also complements the algorithmic re-sults with related products and downloads. This diversity enables query disambiguation by letting users clarify whether they want to buy a product or need support. Clearly, there's also an opportunity for cross-selling and upselling. Best Bets and search analytics in general are as useful in marketing circles as they are in the world of user experience.

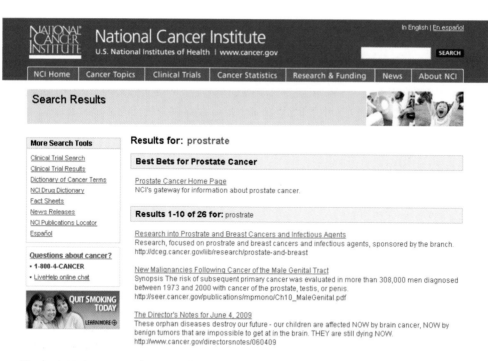

Figure 4-12. *Best Bets at the National Cancer Institute*

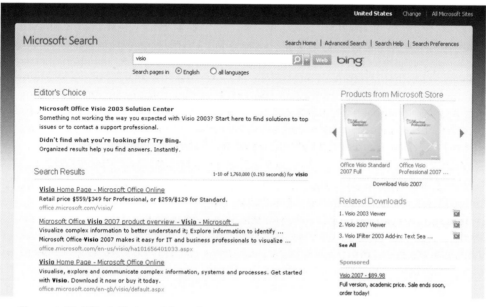

Figure 4-13. *Editor's Choice at Microsoft*

For Best Bets, design considerations include the number and presentation of suggested links and their relationship to algorithmic results. Generally, one to three suggestions per query is sufficient. Ideally, links that appear as Best Bets are removed from the algorithmic list to avoid wasting valuable space with redundant results. And while it's not necessary to spatially separate the two types of results, in the interest of transparency it's helpful to label the Best Bets and visually distinguish them from the natural results.

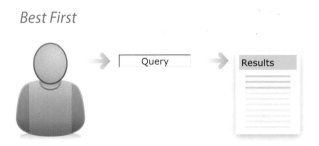

Figure 4-14. *The best first design pattern*

In short, best first is the most universal and important design pattern in search. Its design is intertwingled with other patterns. The first few results must satisfy the simple lookup and support query clarification and refinement, but those results may appear first in autocomplete and may be modified using faceted navigation. Or they may be prequalified with advanced or personalized search. Finally, it's no good delivering the best of the worst. It's impossible for users to find what they need when searching the wrong place, which is why we must study the precarious pattern of federated search.

# FEDERATED SEARCH

By definition, federated search involves the simultaneous search of multiple databases or collections. In intranets, it runs a single query across the staff directory and the subsites of multiple business units. On the Internet, it takes queries where crawlers can't by tapping into dynamic databases of the deep Web. In libraries (Figure 4-15), it lets users search multiple catalogs, collections, databases, and websites all at once.

Federated search may be necessary when managing dynamic content from multiple sources with different data models, but it does present challenges. First and foremost, performance is notoriously slow. As the number and size of collections grow, speed suffers. This is a serious flaw. Plus, the query language may be limited to the lowest common denominator in the face of disparate vocabularies and data models. Sophisticated approaches like faceted navigation may be precluded by federated search.

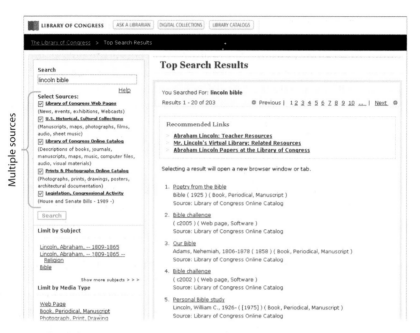

**Figure 4-15.** *Federated search at the Library of Congress*

**Figure 4-16.** *Federated search at Kosmix*

So, before committing to this solution, it's worth reframing the problem. When content is scattered into silos, users don't know where to search. Fragmentation is the root cause. Federated search addresses this problem, but it's not the only way. Instead, we can defragment the content by pulling it all into an integrated index. This may enable fast, powerful, unified queries, but is it still federated search? At this point, our definition needs clarification. Generally, when we talk about "multiple databases or collections," there's a symmetry between the front and back ends. But this needn't be true. Mirroring the technical architecture within the user experience is a design decision. Is it valuable for users to know these resources are from different sources? Is source a more important distinction than topic, format, or date? Will users need to define subsets of collections to search or execute more powerful queries using the native interfaces of individual databases? If the answer to these questions is, "No," federated search may become an antipattern that adds drag to the back end and visual clutter to the front.

That said, federated search can serve as a stepping stone by helping people visualize and play with possible and desirable outcomes. At the Library of Congress, the prospect of a single search across multiple collections was met with some skepticism. Federated search was a first step to get the ball rolling. However, the very next step may involve moving beyond federated search by unifying indexes and embracing a faceted navigation user interface that emphasizes topic and format more than source. Similarly, the alpha version of Boxee (shown in Figure 4-17) is an intriguing first step. Boxee is a social media center that supports multiple sources and formats of videos, music, and pictures from desktop computers, broadcast networks, and the Internet. It's a web-based service designed for big-screen television, and it's a radically federated solution that makes us think differently about how we might find and share media in the not-so-distant future. Boxee is also pretty difficult to use, in part because it spotlights sources rather than focusing on user-friendly ways to search and browse. It's a stepping stone, not a bridge.

In summary, federated search is important because users don't know where to search. Whenever content is fragmented into multiple locations, this pattern merits discussion. However, it's important to focus on the goal, not fixate on the pattern. If it's possible to unify the indexes, that may be the right solution, even if it's not technically federated search.

If source isn't relevant to users, there's no need to highlight it in the results. It may suffice to list source on the detail pages or include it as a metadata field within the faceted navigation display. Indeed, federated search must be carefully integrated with other patterns. Autocomplete and best first will need to draw suggestions from multiple sources. Advanced search may enable database selection, while the complementary modes of ask and browse may be harder to align across multiple sites. But no pattern is more closely tied to federated search than faceted navigation, since it offers users a great way to see and select sources within an integrated model of clarification and refinement.

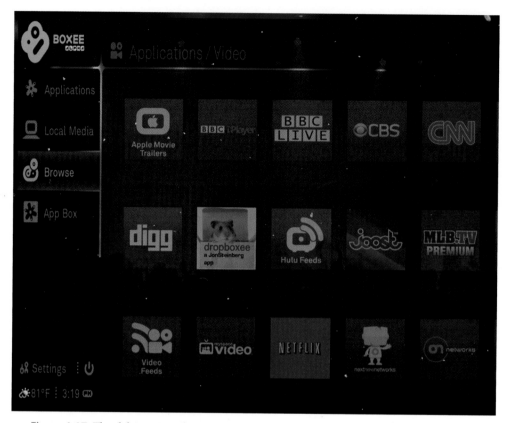

**Figure 4-17.** *The alpha version of Boxee*

## Federated Search

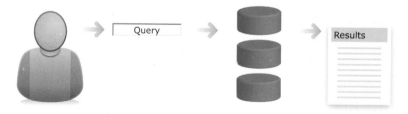

**Figure 4-18.** *The federated search design pattern*

# FACETED NAVIGATION

Also called *guided navigation* and *faceted search*, the faceted navigation model lever-ages metadata fields and values to provide users with visible options for clarifying and refining queries. Faceted navigation is arguably the most significant search innovation of the past decade.[2] It features an integrated, incremental search and browse experi-ence that lets users begin with a classic keyword search and then scan a list of results. It also serves up a custom map (usually to the left of results) that provides insights into the content and its organization and offers a variety of useful next steps. That's where facet-ed navigation proves its power. In keeping with the principles of progressive disclosure and incremental construction, users can formulate the equivalent of a sophisticated Boolean query by taking a series of small, simple steps. Faceted navigation addresses the universal need to narrow. Consequently, this pattern has become nearly ubiquitous in e-commerce, given the availability of structured metadata and the clear business val-ue of improving product findability. Faceted navigation is being deployed rapidly across an impressively wide variety of contexts and platforms. In the world of search, faceted navigation is everywhere.

Figure 4-19 illustrates a successful implementation of faceted navigation as a model for interacting with the catalogs of several academic libraries. This is a good example of a federated search in which source (roughly equivalent to location) is deemphasized relative to subject and format. The consortium's goal is to connect students and faculty with the best materials, regardless of which university owns them. This example also hints at the design challenges. Faceted navigation is not simply a feature to check off a list. Success requires painstaking attention to detail and an appreciation for the vast ar-ray of possibilities for interaction design. For instance, the libraries run collapsible facets down the left. Only the most relevant facets (subject, format, location) are open. Most are closed by default. Each open facet reveals only the top four or five most heavily populated values. This allows for a small facet footprint that frees up plenty of space on the main stage for the results themselves. The number of matching results for each value (shown within parentheses) is a key element of the map, as is the reformulation of search terms and selected values as stacking breadcrumbs, which let users view and modify their current search parameters. This interface is the result of user research, us-ability testing, and iterative design. But it's not the only way.

2 Marti Hearst and her Flamenco project collaborators at UC Berkeley deserve credit for their pioneering research in faceted navigation (*http://flamenco.berkeley.edu/*).

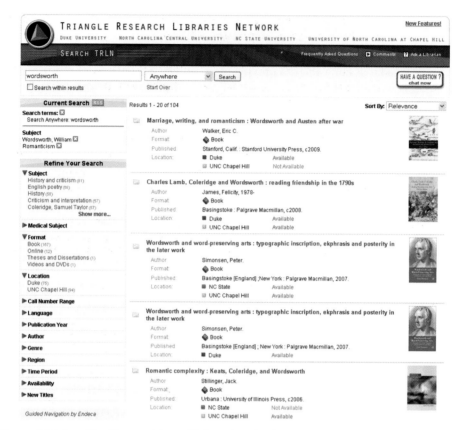

**Figure 4-19.** *Searching library catalogs with faceted navigation*

For instance, applications rely on a mix of *scented widgets* for viewing and interacting with facet values, and some shift facet selectors to the top or right rather than the left.

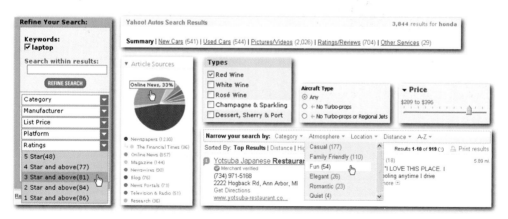

**Figure 4-20.** *A variety of scented widgets*

Presenting facets along the top draws added attention to the narrowing facility. Given massive result sets, this is an effective way to highlight the data structure and draw users into filtering. Top placement may sometimes obscure results and cause clutter, but can work well with image collections like Artist Rising (Figure 4-21) or when only a few facets are needed. It's often useful to allow for flexibility in the number of facets displayed. As shown in Figure 4-22, adaptive facets let controls conform to the content as users shift between categories and drill down within collections. This may be a reason to avoid facets on top. While less visible, facets on the right can work, too, assuming they appear to be controls rather than ads and don't get cut off by narrow browsers. When in doubt, lean toward the de facto standard (left side) and subject different designs to user research and testing.

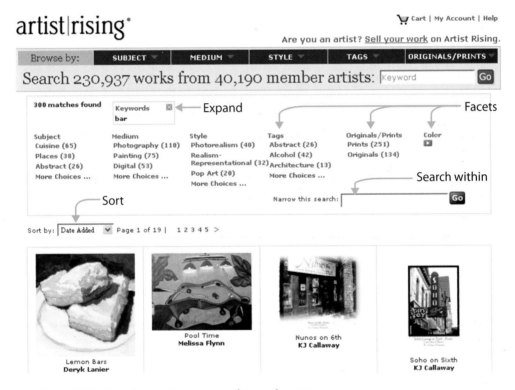

Figure 4-21. *Faceted navigation puts metadata on the map*

**Figure 4-22.** *Amazon's adaptive facets*

In contrast to the relatively mature design space of the desktop Web, mobile is a platform where standards for faceted navigation have yet to emerge. A few research projects such as FaThumb[3] have explored the challenges and possibilities of facet-based interfaces for mobile search. Clearly, tiny screens preclude the established model. There's insufficient space to present facets and values alongside results. Ever the pioneer, Amazon is among the first to design a mainstream application that adds faceted navigation to mobile search. As Figure 4-23 shows, it features an iterative model that requires more steps than ideal, but it's a move in the right direction. As mobile search crosses the chasm, users will expect the features and functions to which they've become accustomed on the desktop, and first and foremost outside of the box, they will absolutely, positively need to narrow.

---

3 A facet-based interface for mobile search. Available at *http://research.microsoft.com/apps/pubs/default.aspx?id=64303.*

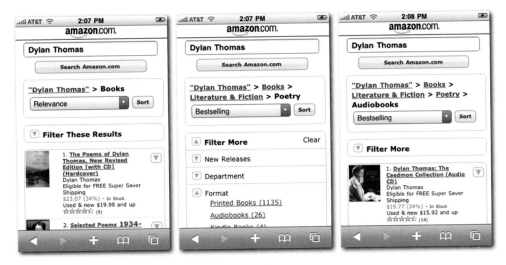

Figure 4-23. *Faceted navigation on Amazon Mobile*

Across all platforms, there are some qualifications and questions worth review. First, we've been using the term "faceted navigation" rather loosely. Formal definitions of facets may exclude simple fields and filters, but discrimination is unwarranted in practice, provided that filters operate independently and users can add or remove them in arbitrary order in concert with the updating of results.

On the other hand, the distinction between faceted navigation and parametric search is relevant. In parametric search applications, users specify their search parameters up front using a variety of controls such as checkboxes, pull-downs, and sliders to construct what effectively is an advanced Boolean query. Unfortunately, it's hard for users to set several parameters at once, especially since many combinations will produce zero results.

Today, it's rare to see pure parametric search, but many applications lean closer to that end of the spectrum than they should. For example, Snooth fails to indicate the number of matching results until after users execute a refined search. The widgets are decidedly unscented and the interface encourages users to modify multiple parameters before query execution. It's a solution that's hard on people but soft on hardware. In other words, it's an unfortunate compromise that sacrifices immediate response to reduce the server load.

Shop in-stock barolo wine
**Results 1-10 of thousands for barolo** *(remove)*

| *Refine Your Search* | ☐ *Include out of stock items* | *Sort By:* | Recommended ▾ |
| *Price* | ◀▶ ⬛ | | *from* US$0 *to* US$138 |
| *Vintage* | ◀▶ | | *wines from* **any vintage** |
| Show Wines Available In | United States ▾ | Postal/Zip | |
| Partner Search ⓘ | ☐ *Winezap* ☐ *Wine-Searcher* | | Refine Search |

**Figure 4-24.** *Parametric problems at Snooth*

At the other extreme, live search applications like Volkswagen UK (Figure 4-25) and Kayak (Figure 4-26) update results dynamically with no submit button and no page refresh. There are some real advantages to this dynamic model, which allows for immediate response, minimal disruption, and elegant transitions. But there are also costs. The Volkswagen UK application takes time to load, and Kayak must use a conspicuous (and somewhat awkward) overlay to call attention to the updated results. Live search applications are like dangerously quiet hybrid vehicles. When the noise disappears, we find it had value. Elegant transitions can reintroduce some useful disruption, but in cases where both results and facets change simultaneously, this becomes a bit tricky.

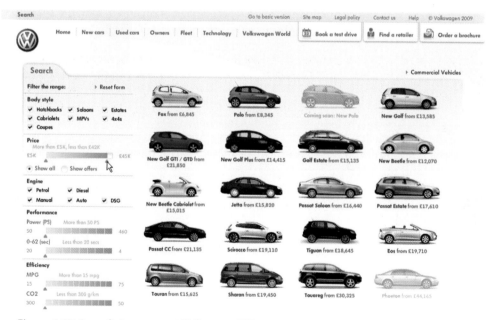

**Figure 4-25.** *Immediate response at Volkswagen UK*

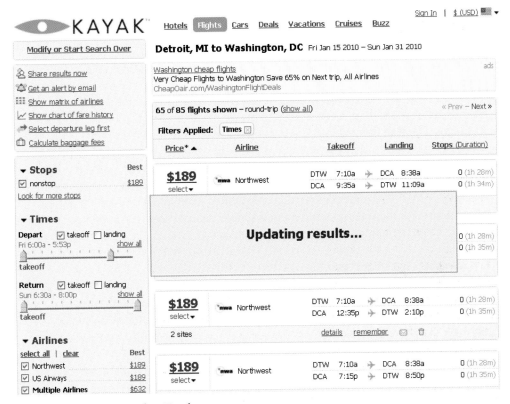

Figure 4-26. *Live search at Kayak*

Of course, as design and technology evolve in concert, we will solve these problems even as new challenges arise. Processors grow faster; people don't. So, we'll need to carefully manage transitions. Meanwhile, faceted navigation will surely adapt to every context and platform because the need to narrow exists at the crossroads of behavior and the box.

### Faceted Navigation

Figure 4-27. *The faceted navigation design pattern*

Faceted navigation is a master pattern. Its deployment impacts all other search patterns and the information architecture as a whole. To oversimplify, there's the Google model and the faceted navigation model. Choosing between these two is a major strategic decision. Determining whether or not faceted navigation is sensible and feasible is among the earliest steps in design. The infrastructure for faceted navigation can enable a tighter relationship between search and browse. It can shape the structure and navigation of the entire site or application. It also changes how we think about autocomplete and best first. It offers a familiar framework for managing the sources of federated search. Plus, its discriminatory power to clarify intent and refine results may offset the need for personalization and advanced search. That said, faceted navigation won't work everywhere. For starters, it's an expensive proposition. The demands on search software and servers are substantial. Also, the metadata infrastructure involves both initial investment and ongoing expense. For these reasons and more, a simpler search model is sometimes better, but it must often be supplemented by advanced search.

## ADVANCED SEARCH

A relative concept, advanced search includes whatever simple search doesn't. It's a pattern that many of us love to hate. Often, advanced search is a clumsy add-on that's rarely used, and it lets engineers and designers take the easy way out. Valuable features that are difficult to integrate into the main interface can be relocated to the ghetto and forgotten. Plus, there's confusion about its purpose. Is it a user-friendly query builder for novices or a power tool for experts? Many interfaces try (and fail) to be both. For instance, isn't it fair to assume that users who understand what "exact phrase" means also know to use quotation marks to specify such a search? The main problem with Boolean isn't the syntax, it's the logic. And even the plain language shown in Figure 4-28 is unlikely to help the few novices who brave the intimidating realm of advanced search.

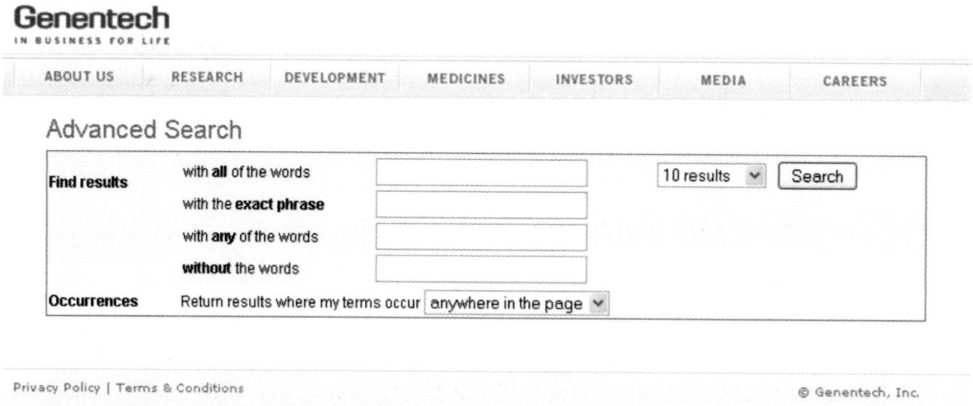

Figure 4-28. *Advanced search at Genentech*

This pattern also suffers from an ignorance of context. Searches are situated. They take place in a space. Having navigated through music to the folk genre, users may want to search without leaving. Scoped search is a pattern that meets this need. There's a risk that users won't see the scope, but overrides in the case of few or no results can help. In most cases, users benefit, because scoped search caters to context. In contrast, advanced search often teleports us to a distant, unfamiliar locale. It's disruptive to flow.

Interestingly, Exalead, shown in Figure 4-29, combines help and advanced search without asking users to leave. A click on Advanced Search launches an interactive menu below the box. It's unconventional and a little clumsy, but definitely worth a look.

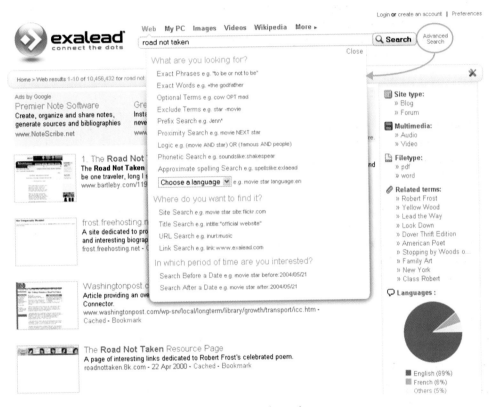

Figure 4-29. *Exalead's integrated Help and Advanced Search*

Despite these difficulties, advanced search isn't only an antipattern. It does help some users learn about the available metadata fields and vocabularies, and offers a path toward greater precision through field-specific searching. Plus, even when we reject the advanced/basic dichotomy and build robust functionality into the main interface, and strive to support contextual queries with scoped search, it's inevitable that some features that are useful for some tasks and for some people will be left out.

In fact, we should worry if they're not. Advanced search offers a safe harbor for edge cases and a clear path to progressive disclosure. For instance, Flickr includes features in advanced search, like limit by license, that simply don't belong on the main stage.

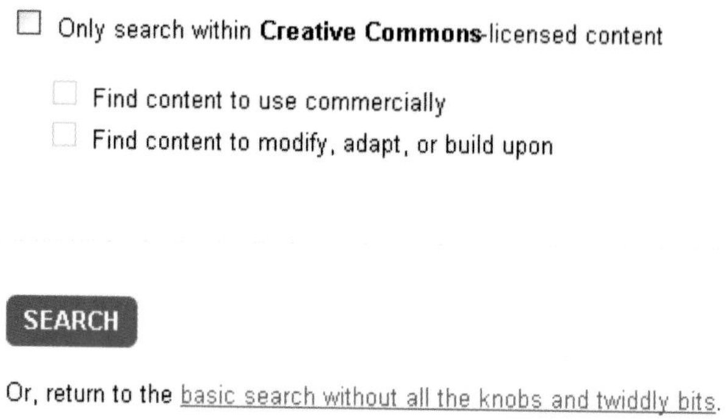

Only search within Creative Commons-licensed content
Find content to use commercially
Find content to modify, adapt, or build upon
SEARCH
Or, return to the basic search without all the knobs and twiddly bits.

Figure 4-30. *Part of Flickr's advanced search interface*

Of equal import, advanced search in concept, if not by name, gets us to think outside the box. What's the basic interface missing? How else might users wish to search? These are the questions that lead to innovations like Midomi's search by singing, GazoPa's discover by drawing, and Etsy's fabulously fun feature, explore by color.

Cart 0 items
Help
Register
Sign In
Etsy
Buy
Sell
Custom
Community
Blog
Your Etsy
Handmade
Search
Advanced Search
Home » Buy » Colors
Colors

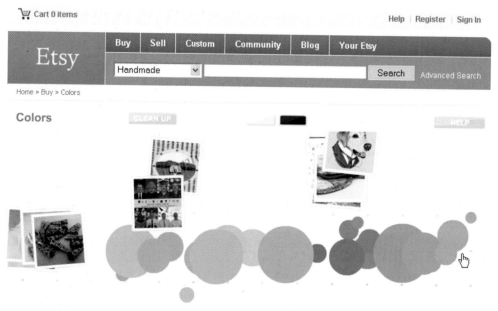

Figure 4-31. *Etsy's explore by color*

In conclusion, advanced search is a pattern on the edge. In practice, it's often abused and rarely used. It can be rendered unnecessary by the narrowing and scoping of faceted navigation and personalization. Yet, like federated search, it invites us to go further in our search for ideas, and serves as a forgiving playground for experiments and exploration.

*Advanced Search*

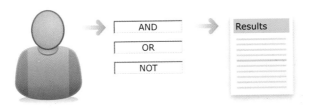

Figure 4-32. *The advanced search design pattern*

## PERSONALIZATION

If you've seen the bow tie–wearing butler in Apple's 1987 Knowledge Navigator video, you know that personalization has been the future of search for decades. Software agents that know what we already know and what we want to know will scour the four corners of the earth for the data that makes a difference. It's a compelling vision that's entirely unrealistic absent a quantum leap in science and technology that enables computers to tap directly into our minds and memories (and understand the meaning of what they find).

So, while it's a worthy ambition, personalization is a hard problem. This inconvenient truth is often obscured by semantics and spin. For starters, personalization is often confused with customization, a simpler model in which users can explicitly modify settings. Customization lets us change color and layout and subscribe to feeds. My Yahoo! and iGoogle are popular examples. Of course, in most applications, users mostly fail to customize. They're too busy. They live with defaults. So designers who count on customization as a crutch will fall flat on their faces. Then there's the spin. Lots of folks have a vested interest in selling the magic of personalization. Enterprise search vendors use it for product differentiation. Web search companies harness it as a Trojan horse to sneak behind firewalls with their targeted ads. After all, it's much easier to use demographic and behavioral data to sell advertising than to improve search, but users will only share their data in return for the promise of better results. And if it's hard for a company like Google, which employs the best and brightest and enjoys unparalleled access to behavioral data, how realistic is it for most sites and applications to personalize search?

OK, enough with the caveats and criticism. Personalization is a pattern worth study. Simple solutions are already well established, and the more sophisticated experiments in similarity computation and social search are intriguing to say the least. Autocomplete is a simple example. As repeat queries are common in many contexts, using search history to inform suggestions is often a good idea. Result reranking based on past post-query behavior is a more complex challenge. A user who repeats a query is likely to click the same result as before. Is it helpful to bring that result to the top? It's worth asking—that is, if we have the behavioral data and the technology to support analysis and action.

Otherwise, we may find the right balance by employing recommendation engines to search for similarity. The most famous of these is Amazon's "Customers Who Bought This Item Also Bought This" feature. It's not perfect. It's heavily influenced by publication date, since we often buy unrelated books together that are popular at the same time. It's not personalization but a form of collaborative filtering that's centered on an item, not an individual. But it does encourage pearl growing, and it's a repeatable solution to a common problem. It's a great search pattern, and music recommendation services like Last.fm have successfully interwoven this approach with individual preferences and similar tastes. Sometimes, personalization really does work like magic.

Figure 4-33. *Support for pearl growing at Amazon*

But Amazon's true personalization is less useful and less used than its collaborative filters. Mining search, navigation, and purchase history to derive helpful, personalized suggestions isn't easy. Results are skewed when we shop for others and buy a bra for grandma. But that's not the crux of the matter. The core problem is that what we wanted yesterday or last year often fails to predict our interests and wishes today and tomorrow.

How can software know what we need now? In search, the query affords a peek at intent. History may offer a hint, and we may improve results with a little help from our friends. In fact, social search is a major area of inquiry in academic circles and an intriguing, albeit immature, pattern in practice. At LinkedIn, results are sorted by degrees of separation. Answers from friends are followed by those from friends of a friend (Figure 4-35).

Figure 4-34. *Personalization at Amazon*

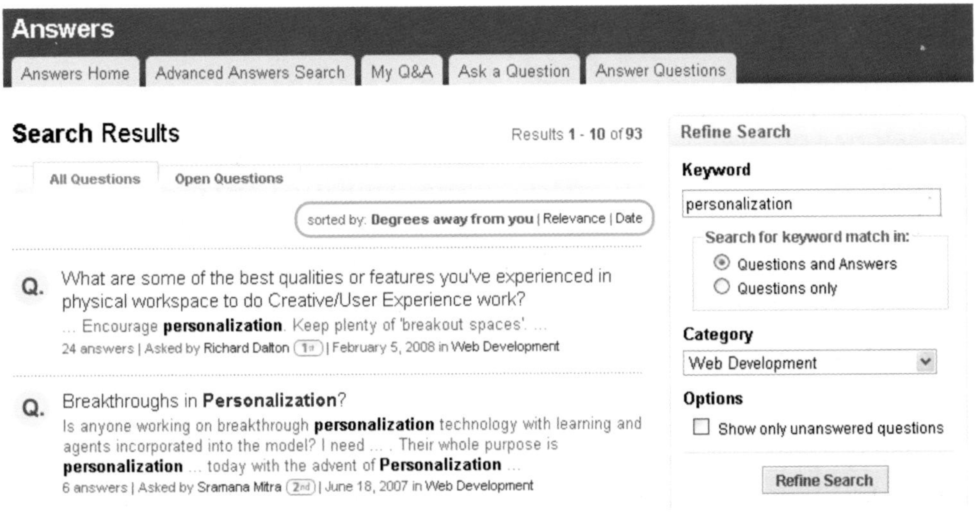

Figure 4-35. *Social search at LinkedIn*

At Twitter, search ignores our friends. Results are sorted solely by time. In contrast, FriendFeed lets us limit queries to our social networks. And therein lies the question: can the personal insights and experience of our friends beat the wisdom of the crowd? The answer is, of course, it depends. The size and composition of the network is a key variable. So is the nature of the question. A tightly knit circle of teenagers may rely heavily on social search for music, fashion, and restaurant recommendations, but similar searches may fall flat for a diverse, international network of executives. For some questions, our friends know us best, but for most queries, there's strength in numbers.

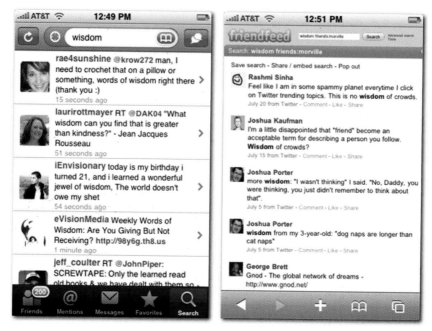

**Figure 4-36.** *Social searches on Twitter and FriendFeed*

So, it's worth asking again: how can software know what we need now? The mobile platform has part of the answer in the form of location awareness. Our current location, in concert with a query (or selection of an application), offers insight into intent and a smart default for sort order. Indeed, even our choice of platform is a clue. A desktop query for "vegetarian" is likely a lookup, but on the iPhone, a local search for restaurants is a good guess. Google Mobile plays it safe by covering both angles. Similarly, simply launching SitorSquat (Figure 4-37) clearly indicates searcher intent: find me the nearest public toilet, stat!

In the digital domain, using the entry point for search as an input for personalization is also an area of inquiry. The most obvious solution is scoped search, covered under the advanced search pattern. Less obvious is an idea popularized by John Battelle and shown in Figure 4-38. If we know where a user came from or how he got here, can we further personalize his experience by embedding recommendations within each result? This extension to contextual search is hardly a pattern, but it's an interesting question to ponder.

Figure 4-37. *Personalizing search by location*

Figure 4-38. *Searchblog's personalized referrals*

In short, personalization is a dish best served simple. Only in limited contexts will past performance predict desired future results. The query is the clearest and most timely signal of intent. It's a concise expression of what users need right now. History, social data, and location (online and off) can sometimes boost that signal, but for practical and ethical reasons, these personal algorithms should be transparent and open to override. When it works, personalization can play well with other patterns. In particular, it informs the suggestions of autocomplete and the algorithms of best first. Often, however, personalization must take a back seat to explicit, dynamic customization in the form of faceted navigation. After all, interactions with facets are the closest we come to the reference interview and what Google cofounder Sergey Brin calls the ultimate personalized search engine: the librarian.

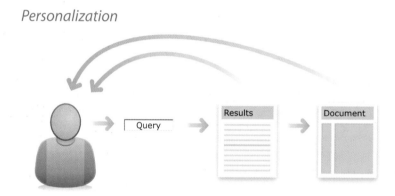

Figure 4-39. *The personalization design pattern*

# PAGINATION

How should we display search results? The next few patterns seek an answer. Since most queries produce too many results for one screen, pagination is a common solution. Google established the most popular pattern in the form of 10 blue links. And while competitors such as Microsoft's Bing are busy decrying the end of this model, it's still alive and kicking as the dominant standard across desktop, web, and mobile platforms.

Of course, the 10 blue links don't really stand alone. Google's results page is a complex, high-density interface. Designers are forced to count every pixel, because every pixel counts. Features include format filters along the top, dual boxes for query refinement, a variety of tools and advanced search options, invitations to explore related searches, and a pagination control for accessing paged content. Last but not least, there are *snippets*.

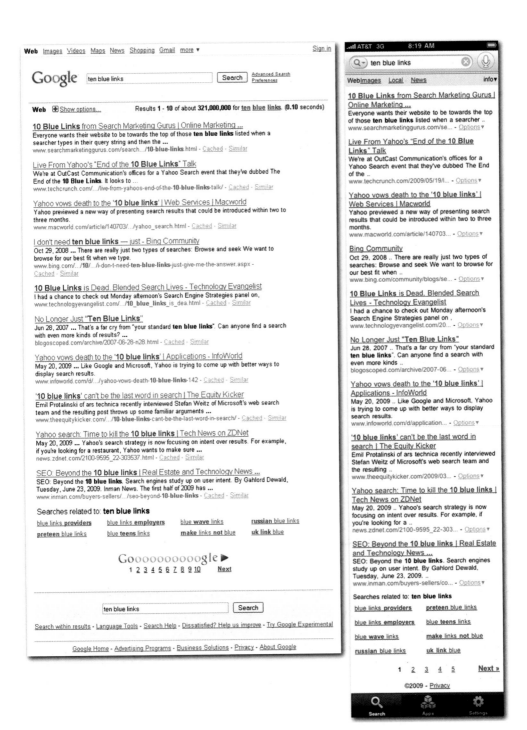

Figure 4-40. *Ten blue links*

Snippets are the heart and soul of search results. To pinch a phrase from multitouch, the content is the interface. The snippet reveals the *aboutness* of each result while also serving as the *link* to live and cached versions and to similar results. A purple link means you've already visited, an important and helpful clue for determining the next click. The two lines of text are selected for optimal scent. They provide a concise summary of the result or a brief excerpt with the keywords in context. A URL offers hints about the source and subject of the result. And throughout the snippet, query keywords are **highlighted** to reveal the reason for inclusion. That's a lot of work for a simple snippet.

Live From Yahoo's "End of the **10 Blue Links**" Talk
We're at OutCast Communication's offices for a Yahoo Search event
that they've dubbed The End of the **10 Blue Links**. It looks to ...
www.techcrunch.com/.../live-from-yahoos-end-of-the-**10-blue-links**-talk/
- Cached - Similar

Figure 4-41. *A Google snippet*

Bing, shown in Figure 4-42, takes snippets a step further by presenting additional text and links from the destination site whenever a user hovers over a particular search result.

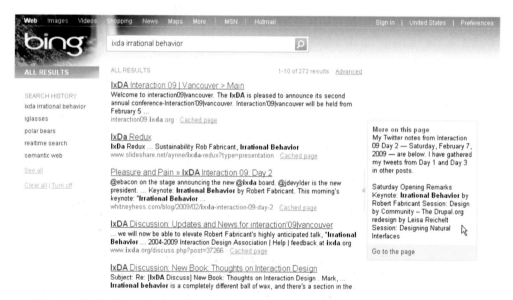

Figure 4-42. *Bing's preview feature*

Of course, the anatomy of a snippet must adapt to fit each platform, format, and context. In mobile, snippets must be short. In reference and news and enterprise applications, URLs may be useless. And for images and video, a picture's worth a thousand words.

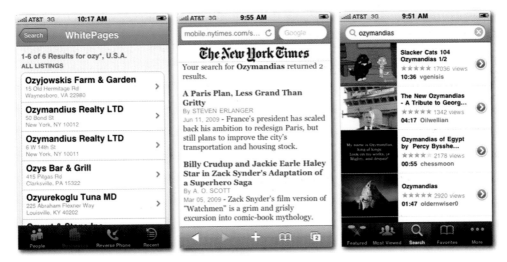

Figure 4-43. *Snippet diversity*

A linear list isn't the only way to organize results. As Figure 4-44 illustrates, the television and movie discovery service Jinni uses size (and layout) to show sort order.

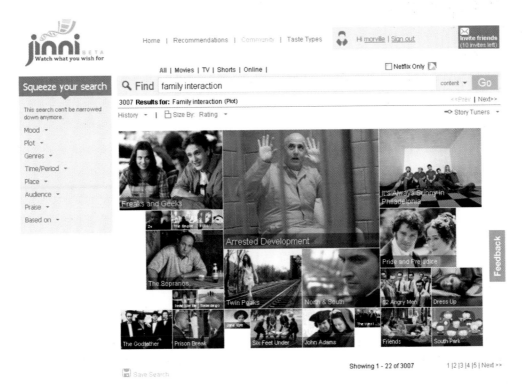

Figure 4-44. *Size by rating at Jinni*

In e-commerce, photos of each product are important. So is choice. At Yahoo! Shopping, users can choose whether they see 15, 30, or 45 results in list or grid view. They also have a wide variety of sort options and can select multiple items for a side-by-side comparison.

**Figure 4-45.** *Result customization at Yahoo! Shopping*

Despite all this flexibility, disruption is an inherent problem of pagination. When users advance to the next set of results, the page refresh often disrupts flow. Inline paging is one solution. At Endless.com, for instance, when users advance to the next result page, the old snippets fade out and new ones appear. The rest of the interface stays stable. The user feels like she never leaves the page. However, after scrolling down through results, there's still a disconcerting jump from page bottom to top. Nothing's perfect!

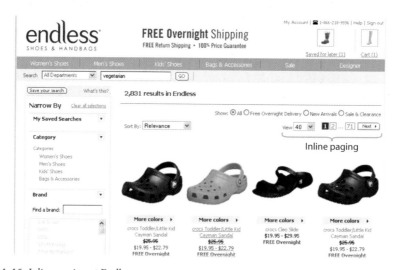

**Figure 4-46.** *Inline paging at Endless.com*

Several solutions are currently employed in mobile. Apple's iTunes offers to Show 25 More at the end of each list. Amazon abolishes paging with virtual scrolling. Progressive loading ensures that the first few results are shown immediately, then, as users scroll down, more results load automatically. Kayak appears to load all matching flights, but sort and filter options are available to refine results and avoid endless scrolling.

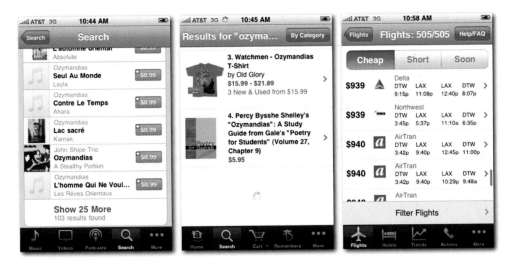

Figure 4-47. *Mobile pagination patterns*

Infinite scroll and inline paging offer clear benefits, but they come at a cost. First, they're simply more expensive to implement. Second, they may initially confuse users who have become used to the standard model. Third, they may frustrate attempts to bookmark or share a link to a specific set of results. Don't forget the power of the page!

Clearly, the pattern of pagination is linked to the composition of the snippet. We must find a balance between the richness of each snippet and the number of results per page. That is, unless our application affords the freedom to try something unorthodox, like a zooming user interface (ZUI) that positions all results within an infinite virtual desktop.

**Figure 4-48.** *Hard Rock's zooming user interface*

In summary, careful attention to pagination delivers results. That's the bottom line. Snippets are central, serving as both content and interface. But one snippet will not fit all. The ideal composition is shaped by platform, format, and context. Flexible sort and filter options are also important. While best first defines the default, users deserve control. That's the genius of faceted navigation. Incremental clarification and refinement reduce results until the need for paging and scrolling virtually disappears.

### Pagination

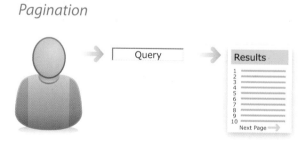

**Figure 4-49.** *The pagination design pattern*

# STRUCTURED RESULTS

Increasingly, our uniform ranks of ordered blue links are being infiltrated by rich snippets and structured results that dig deeper into the data so users don't have to. Google made this mainstream by embedding maps, images, stock charts, and more into its results. Google also experiments perpetually with options like timeline view and with new projects like Google Public Data, which makes it easy to find and visually compare statistical data.

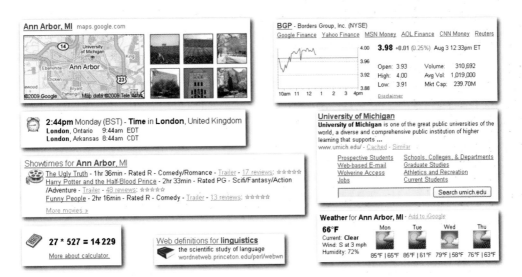

Figure 4-50. *Google's structured results*

What's the optimal format for this type of result? Will a classic snippet suffice, or is there a better way? Can we summarize or surface data with an image or chart? Can we subtract clicks by adding answers? These are the questions we must ask. Of course, users' queries are important, too, since the desired output may depend upon structured input. It's a model that only works well when we can reliably infer user intent.

It's also a pattern that challenges boundaries. When is search not a search? When it's a calculator or a dictionary or an application we have yet to define. Wolfram Alpha strays well outside the box. Natural language queries and curated data are subjected to linguistic analysis and computation. Results include tables, charts, formulas, visualizations, and dynamic controls. It's not really a search engine at all; it's a computational knowledge engine. Its results are meant to be answers. But where do we draw the line?

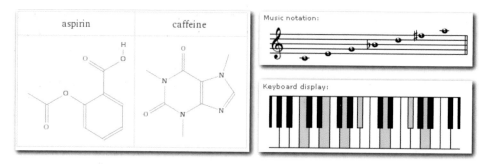

**Figure 4-51.** *Wolfram Alpha's structured results*

On the search side, subtle visualizations invite attention and analysis. At Newssift, shown in Figure 4-52, emphasis is placed on identifying patterns, trends, and relationships. It's about the discovery of meaning. Structure isn't a function of individual answers; rather, it's a way to understand and manage large sets of results.

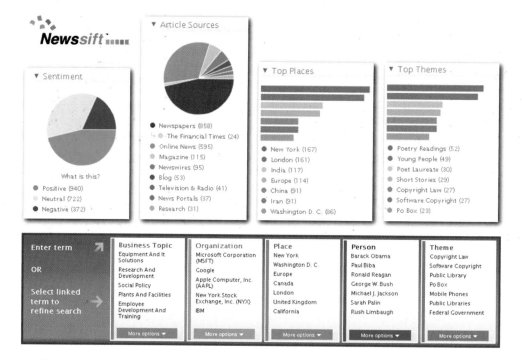

**Figure 4-52.** *Visual facet widgets at Newssift*

Meanwhile, the distinctions between analytics, business intelligence, decision support, text mining, and exploratory search continue to blur. Powerful queries and visualizations that were limited to structured data are being applied to multiformat collections and unstructured text. Endeca, for instance, is pioneering an approach called *guided summarization* (shown in Figure 4-53), which integrates faceted navigation with dynamic visualizations that engage users in a rich dialog with their data. While search may still start in a box, the potential applications of modern tools are all over the map.

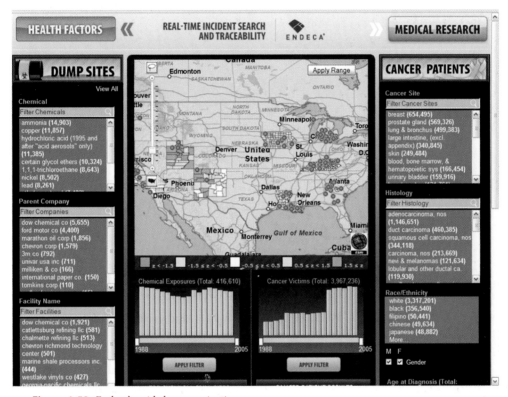

Figure 4-53. *Endeca's guided summarization*

In summary, structure is reshaping our results. Search applications are simply better when they swap a picture for a thousand words or take users one step deeper into the data. And this pattern plays well with others. While rich snippets may not appear in autocomplete, they're often part of best first. Features like movies, maps, and weather surely benefit from personalization, and faceted navigation offers a good model for managing text as structured data. Of course, when the response is an answer or a new frame for our question, we must wonder: is this really what we talk about when we talk about search?

### Structured Results

**Figure 4-54.** *The structured results design pattern*

## ACTIONABLE RESULTS

But enough talk already. We want action. We need results. That's what actionable results are all about. Why list a link when we can lend a hand? First, we must ask what users want to do with their results. The most common tasks are print, save, and share.

Yahoo! Search Pad (Figure 4-55) manages them all. It's a handy application that tracks the results we visit. We can add notes, print, save, and share the annotated list of search results via Delicious, Facebook, Twitter, or by using a custom URL. Searchme pioneered a more visual model with similar functionality (Figure 4-56), which lets users drag and drop results into shareable search stacks.

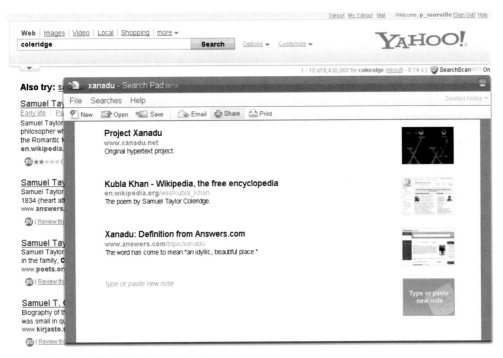

Figure 4-55. *Yahoo! Search Pad*

Figure 4-56. *Drag results to stacks at Searchme*

Users may also wish to vote, rate, and comment on results. This is clearly a core feature of Digg, a social news website that proves the power of actionable results. As founder Kevin Rose explained, "Once we added Ajax, activity went through the roof…the ease of the 'one-click and you're done' made all the difference in the world." Google is now experimenting with this type of feature. When signed into Google, users can remove, promote, or comment upon individual results. For now, it's considered a personalization feature, but Google is surely storing the social data with an eye toward public results.

Figure 4-57. *Actionable results at Digg and Google*

Tools that help users to manage results are a good idea, but we can often do better by seeing the goal beyond the search. Hulu, for instance, doesn't simply list results. There's a play button in every snippet, so we can watch TV shows and movies with a single click.

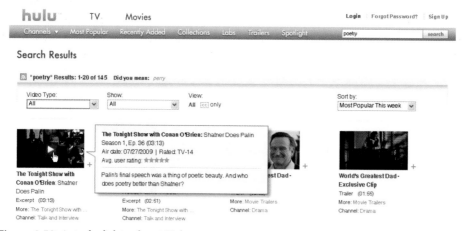

Figure 4-58. *A single click to play at Hulu*

Yahoo! has integrated structured and actionable results into its main search experience by presenting expanded snippets for top results when possible. This strategy fits nicely with the best first pattern. As Figure 4-59 illustrates, music fans are able to play songs and watch videos without leaving the results page.

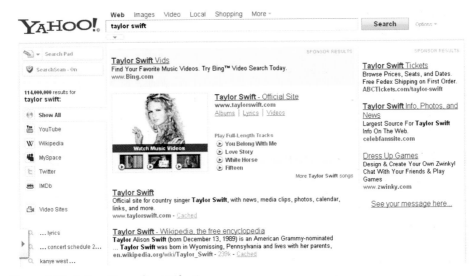

Figure 4-59. *Actionable results at Yahoo!*

Similarly, Spotlight Search on the iPhone isn't just a way to find files fast. It's also an efficient and elegant way to launch applications and make phone calls. Google Mobile goes a step further by integrating single-click phone and map features. And Apple's iTunes lets us play songs and buy music without having to leave our results.

Figure 4-60. *Actionable results in mobile applications*

In short, actionable results are the next step for users and for search. We must stay focused on the goal and design for results beyond results. Clearly, this pattern can be integrated with most others. For instance, actions can begin with autocomplete. On the iPhone, users can launch an application before the query is whole. It's good to get an early start. The real trick is knowing where to end. Do we embed the basic features of other applications in our search software? Do we create hooks from our results into other software that offers a more robust feature set? Implementation is tricky, but it's worth the extra effort, because real-world goals require that we think and act outside the box.

*Actionable Results*

Figure 4-61. *The actionable results design pattern*

# UNIFIED DISCOVERY

Search rarely stands alone. In most contexts, users move between modes of searching, browsing, and asking. They don't bother about borders. We can learn from their example by embracing the pattern of patterns known as *unified discovery*. Sometimes it's about making the modes work together. Other times it's about merging modes. For instance, Yahoo! Glue Pages are specialized, visually appealing, browsable search results. They're Google and Wikipedia, gateway and destination, search and browse all rolled into one.

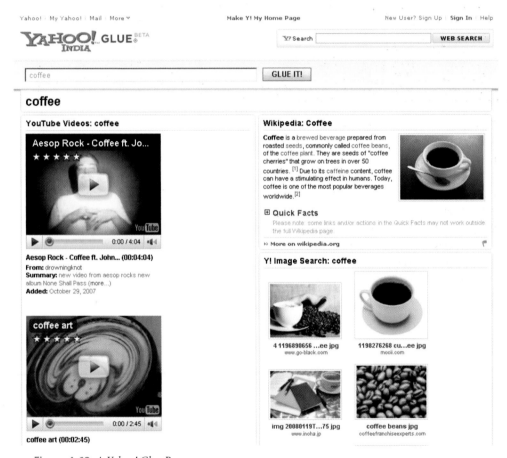

Figure 4-62. *A Yahoo! Glue Page*

We're also making browse more like search. At Lands' End, there's little difference between search results and a gallery page (see Figure 4-63) that results from browse. Pagination and the sort and display options are handled the same way. Plus, even as we browse the product taxonomy, faceted navigation options appear to the left.

**Figure 4-63.** *Blending browse and search at Lands' End*

Unfortunately, Lands' End fails to integrate modes in other important ways. There's no scoped search, so we can't limit our queries to women's sweaters or boys' shoes. And, although it does offer a useful Live Help feature, the collaboration is hindered because, as Figure 4-64 shows, we can't easily share our results with the representative.

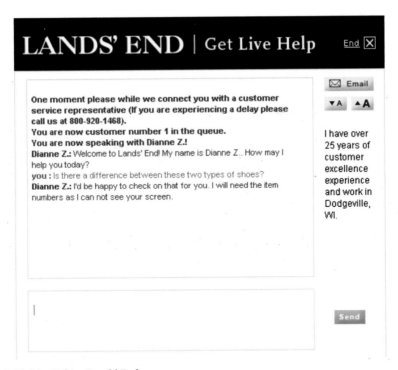

Figure 4-64. *Live Help at Lands' End*

One way to make the modes work together is by leveraging category matches. When a user's query partially or exactly matches a category label, we have a choice. One option, shown in Figure 4-65, is to highlight the category match and present results as usual. That's a reasonable solution for a partial match. However, users may not notice the category link or understand what it represents. An alternative is to jump to the category page, also shown in Figure 4-65. This requires an exact match or the ability to map a near match onto a single category. In such cases, an override option that lets users run their original query is helpful, since the category page may not always be the desired result.

A third option is evident at Amazon (shown in Figure 4-66), where category matches are integrated as facets to the left of results. This is a balanced solution that keeps the user in search while leveraging the structure of the browsable taxonomy.

Partial category match "shower chair"

Exact category match "showers"

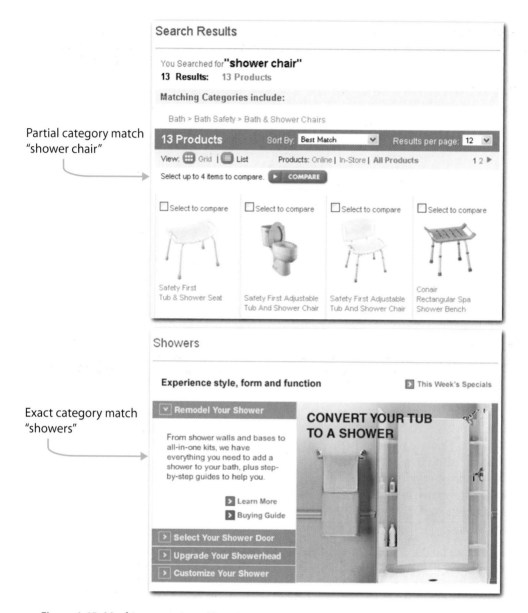

Figure 4-65. *Matching categories at Home Depot*

Of course, Amazon is the champion when it comes to making search and browse work together. As Figure 4-67 shows, while we browse departments, scoped search offers to limit our queries to that section. At Amazon, whether we search or browse first, we can always switch to the other mode without losing our place.

Figure 4-66. *Category match at Amazon*

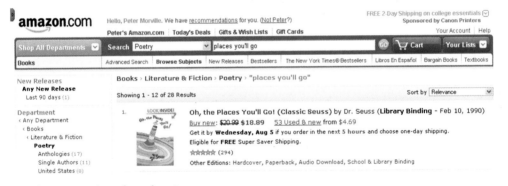

Figure 4-67. *Scoped search at Amazon*

Unified discovery provides a framework in which to integrate patterns. For each search pattern, we should ask how it might relate to browse. Autocomplete and best first might automatically feature category matches. Personalized search may be informed by our current location and browsing history. And, of course, the key fields and filters of faceted navigation should be aligned with categories and the overall information architecture.

*Unified Discovery*

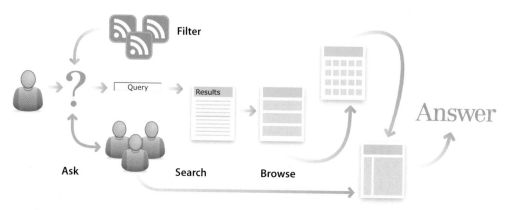

**Figure 4-68.** *The unified discovery design pattern*

# THE END OF THE BEGINNING

In this chapter, we've explored 10 major search patterns. It's a start, but our inventory isn't nearly complete. Christopher Alexander and his colleagues compiled 253 architectural patterns for houses, gardens, neighborhoods, and villages. We're not even close. Our best patterns have yet to emerge, and we're in dire need of a map that shows how they fit together. The task is particularly difficult because our patterns are such a motley crew. Some fall squarely within the boxes of interaction design or information architecture, while others are boundary spanners that blur the lines between user experience, content strategy, knowledge management, and search. These patterns run the gamut from tactical to strategic, and therein lies our challenge: we must pay attention to spelling and syntax while simultaneously telling a good story. The writing doesn't always come easy. In fact, we're often at a loss for words. Our vocabulary for designing and describing interactions is limited and limiting. It imprisons our imagination. We can do better, so we must seek new words and weave them together most densely, because:

> *in search*
>
> *as in poetry,*
>
> *less is more,*
>
> *patterns slow time,*
>
> *and discovery springs*
>
> *from rhythm and rhyme.*

# 5

# Engines of Discovery

*Let your hook always be cast. In the pool where you least expect it, there will be fish.*

—Ovid

*Serendipity* refers to an accidental yet desirable discovery. It plays a surprising role. Alexander Fleming's failure to disinfect cultures of bacteria before leaving for vacation led to the discovery of penicillin. Archimedes figured out how to measure the volume of irregularly shaped objects by taking a bath. And Columbus found America by sailing for India. LSD, Uranus, Viagra, safety glass, infrared radiation, microwave ovens, inkjet printers, Corn Flakes, and chocolate chip cookies are all accidental discoveries. It's amazing what we find while searching for something else. In fact, search and serendipity often travel together. Discovery requires that we move beyond what we know. Ironically, the most frustrating journeys can lead to the best and least expected destinations. As the dictionary evangelist Erin McKean remarked, "Serendipity is when you find things you weren't looking for because finding what you are looking for is so damned difficult."

This reveals a tension in search between relevance and interestingness. The most interesting (and valuable) results aren't always the most relevant. Often, the best answers lie just beyond the edges of what we know to seek. In this ambiguity lies the promised land of personalization, collaborative filtering, recommender systems, and discovery engines. But software algorithms take us only so far. We must also rely on an idiosyncratic mix of subscriptions and memberships that veil the signal in noise. And, of course, exposure to the right publications and discussions is only half the puzzle. Insight requires that we make strange connections that bridge contexts and categories. It's easy to copy from competitors, but mapping an e-commerce feature to the unique requirements of mobile social search requires vision and ingenuity. Colorful stories and surprising examples pave the path to serendipity, but our minds are the real engines of discovery.

# CATEGORY

Earlier, we defined the primary categories of search as web, e-commerce, enterprise, desktop, mobile, social, and real time. Mostly, we labor within one of these boxes, but that doesn't mean we can't learn from the others. For instance, IBM offers an inspiring case study in applying ideas across categories. In the earliest days of Web 2.0, folks at IBM saw the potential of social software to transform knowledge management within the enterprise. Long before Enterprise 2.0 entered our vocabulary, researchers at IBM had rolled out Dogear, an enterprise-class social bookmarking and tagging tool similar to Delicious. The intranet team also deployed blogs, wikis, and the award-winning BluePages employee directory. While executives at other firms fretted about the dangers of tagging, IBM's w3 was successfully increasing the productivity, collaboration, and innovation of its massive global workforce. The IBM team also launched an enterprise social search project to harness all that social data to improve search and social networking. Unfortunately, the first attempt was a flop. As shown in Figure 5-1, users could find people, discussions, and news relevant to their queries simply by clicking the tabs along the top of each result set. But nobody clicked the tabs. Site analytics suggested a very low interest in this social content.

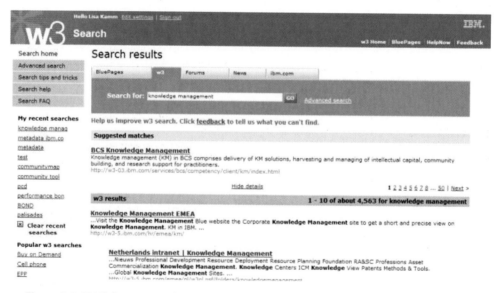

Figure 5-1. *IBM's first version of enterprise social search*

To its credit, the team didn't quit. Instead, it tried again. In the second version, shown in Figure 5-2, the interface brought sample social content right to the surface. Users got a glimpse of relevant and popular content in blogs, wikis, forums, news, and the employee directory. Suddenly, clickthroughs skyrocketed. Users were intensely interested in this social content. They simply hadn't known what they were missing. With this success in its pocket, the team began integrating social data, such as ratings and tag frequency, directly into the algorithms for enterprise search. A page that's been bookmarked, for instance, receives a boost. Similar to Google's PageRank, this form of social search improves both relevance and user satisfaction. Together, these advances in enterprise social search make IBM a better business and a better place to work.

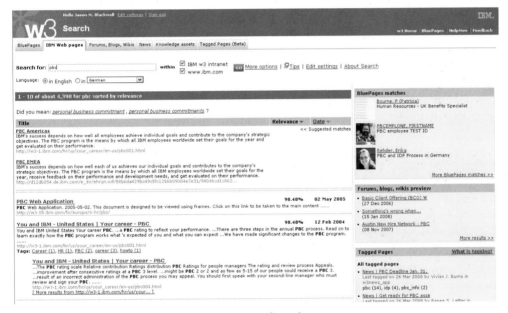

*Figure 5-2. IBM's second version of enterprise social search*

Of course, not everyone has the team and technology of IBM. It's vital to fit the engine to the institution. At Washtenaw Community College, for example, it made sense to go with Google. By selecting an easy-to-deploy solution, its small web services team reserved the time and budget necessary to invest in an information architecture and visual identity overhaul. Plus, it integrated search into the new framework quite nicely, and managed to add Best Bets or "Featured Results" for many of the most common queries.

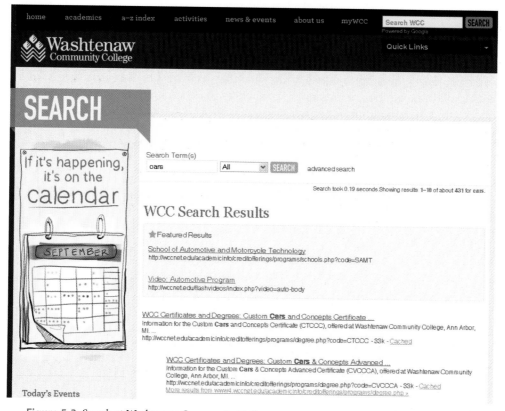

Figure 5-3. *Search at Washtenaw Community College*

Most of the examples we encounter on a daily basis don't come with a backstory. But that doesn't mean we can't learn from each one, provided we allow for the differences. For instance, the faceted search of Cisco.com, shown in Figure 5-4, offers insights for folks working on intranets. In particular, the document type and task facets are eminently transferable.

In the local category, Citysearch, shown in Figure 5-5, offers a great example of actionable results. Since the options appear on result rollover, they don't clutter the screen, but are easy to discover.

In real time, Twitter, shown in Figure 5-6, provides dynamic updates, letting us see how many matching tweets have been posted since we started searching. Results are presented within the framework of the main user interface, so people can stay in the flow and keep on tweeting on.

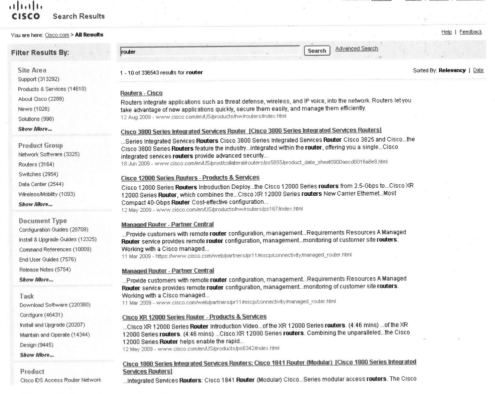

Figure 5-4. *Faceted search at Cisco*

Figure 5-5. *Actionable results at Citysearch*

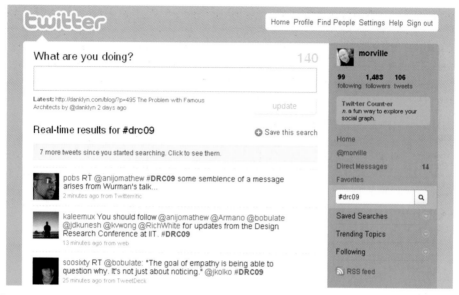

Figure 5-6. *Twitter's real-time search*

In contrast, TweetDeck is a desktop application that makes it easy to organize updates into multiple columns by source, group, format, and search string. Users can modify the refresh rate of each column and opt for visual and/or audio notifications.

Figure 5-7. *Real-time search with TweetDeck*

Research products designed for libraries, universities, and other institutional subscribers represent an interesting but well-hidden category of search applications. Access generally requires membership, subscription, or an onsite visit to a public or college library. Historically, these research products have been designed for the librarians who purchase them rather than for the students and faculty who use them, but a shift toward user-centered design is underway.

ProQuest Smart Search, shown in Figure 5-8, is an innovation designed for end users. Since most folks aren't comfortable extracting controlled vocabulary terms from a thesaurus, ProQuest developed technology that analyzes a user's query, maps the terms to the controlled vocabulary, and then offers suggestions for related topics and publications.

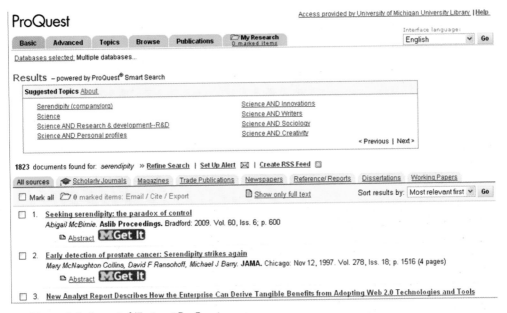

Figure 5-8. *Suggested Topics at ProQuest*

LexisNexis Academic, a massive law, business, and news database, adds its own twist to the faceted navigation model with a flexible panel, shown in Figure 5-9, that users can drag to the right to accommodate long facet values, such as the titles of law reviews, journals, and cases.

EBSCO's visual search interface to the PsycINFO database, shown in Figure 5-10, offers an attractive alternative to a traditional faceted navigation display. It may not be the right approach for most mainstream search applications, but it does inspire us to think outside the box.

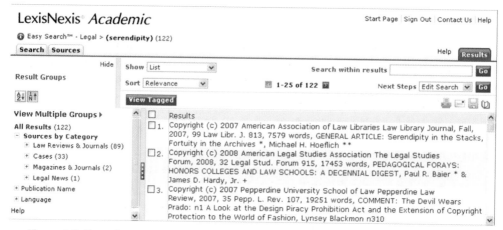

Figure 5-9. *Faceted navigation at LexisNexis*

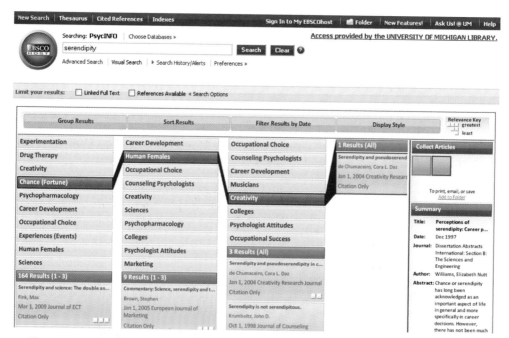

Figure 5-10. *EBSCO's visual search of PsycINFO*

In short, whether we're focused on web, e-commerce, enterprise, desktop, mobile, social, or real time, we can still borrow patterns and spark ideas by looking outside our category.

# TOPIC

It's also worth wandering the nooks and crannies of vertical search. In health, for instance, GoPubMed shows what can be done with a highly structured knowledge base. Users can view charts and graphs for any set of search results. This is the sort of feature that can spark an idea for a search application in a totally different category or topic.

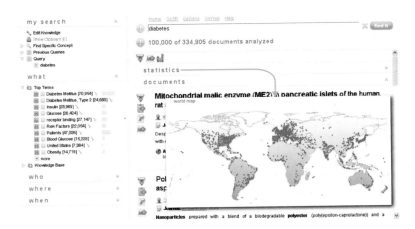

*Figure 5-11. Viewing statistics at GoPubMed*

In food, Epicurious serves up a mouth-watering faceted navigation model that lets users refine by main ingredient, meal, course, and cuisine. Plus, Epicurious has integrated its facets into an iPhone application, so users can flick to filter.

*Figure 5-12. Web and mobile applications of Epicurious*

Urbanspoon delivers a very different food-finding experience. In addition to offering a variety of search, browse, and social navigation options, this application lets us shake our iPhones to tap serendipity. Search as a slot machine is an entertaining form of discovery.

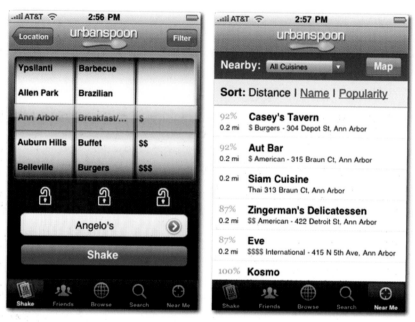

Figure 5-13. *Shake to search with Urbanspoon*

Customer support is another vertical to watch. For instance, Dopplr offers an unusually rich experience by using a third-party application called Get Satisfaction.

Figure 5-14. *Customer satisfaction at Dopplr*

Unfortunately, it's hidden under Help, since Dopplr doesn't connect to this content from the site search. Still, done right, hosted niche applications can take some pressure off search.

# FORMAT

Search applications that are focused on a single format can also open our eyes. Sometimes, it's just about fun. After an exhausting debate about sort order options, contemplating the chaotic piles of oSkope's visual search application can deliver valuable comic relief.

Figure 5-15. *oSkope's visual search*

But a focus on format can also uncover more adaptable solutions. Simply searching bookmarks at Delicious, shown in Figure 5-16, reveals an elegant integration of auto-suggest, filter by tag, and result visualization that could be profitably redeployed in many categories and contexts.

MrTaggy, an experiment in web search and exploration, also relies on social tags rather than full-text content to drive its ranking algorithms. Its novel user interface supports relevance feedback by inviting people to vote up or down on tags and individual results.

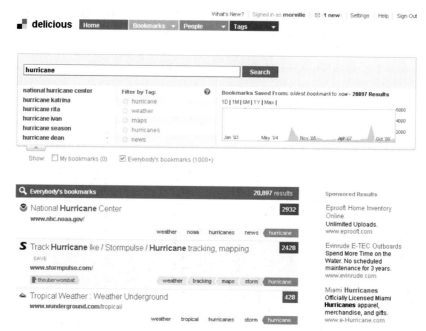

**Figure 5-16.** *Search results at Delicious*

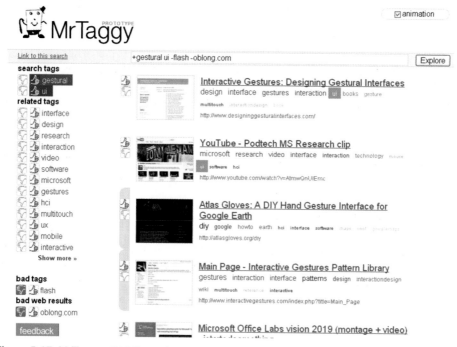

**Figure 5-17.** *MrTaggy, a PARC experiment*

Shopping for just the right colors of paint offers a very different challenge in which keywords are only a small piece of the puzzle. Olympic has developed a Paint a Photo application that not only provides myriad ways to search and browse colors, but also lets users drag and drop to see how their selections might match.

**Figure 5-18.** *Mixing colors at Olympic*

In clothing, Modista makes it easy to search by color and shape (Figure 5-19). Users simply click on an item they like in order to find more items like it. It's a fast, fluid iterative and interactive experience. Modista actually manages to make shopping and searching fun.

Over in the world of social networking, LinkedIn leverages the structured data of people's profiles to enable query refinement (Figure 5-20). Since these advanced search options are presented alongside results, it's easier for users to calibrate their narrowing query for just the right level of precision.

Working on a format-specific search application can present fascinating challenges. Surprisingly, the constraint of a single content type affords new freedoms. We need not worry about entire classes of content and query types. And when working solely with photographs, for example, there are all sorts of specialized search and interaction models to explore. Focus begets freedom begets discovery, which is why single-format search is fertile ground for innovation. We can all learn a lot by surveying these applications.

Figure 5-19. *Search by color and shape at Modista*

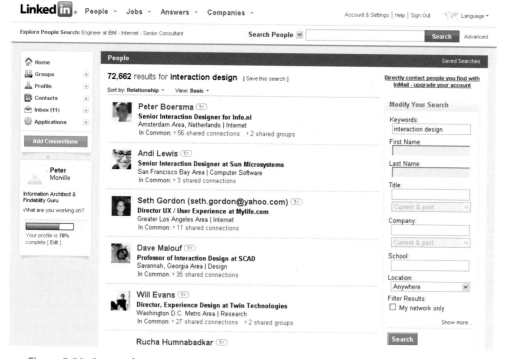

Figure 5-20. *Query refinement at LinkedIn*

# AUDIENCE

Tuning applications to the needs of a niche audience is a trickier proposition. As we discussed in Chapter 2, search expertise and domain expertise influence information-seeking behavior more than demographics. That said, there are a growing number of audience-specific search engines. In China, there's a "Baidu for Kids" and a "Baidu Elderly Search." The latter features large fonts, fewer graphics, clicks over text entry, and an emphasis on topics of interest to retirees. In Israel, a kosher version of Google called Koogle is optimized for Hebrew-speaking Orthodox Jews. Its index omits sexually explicit and religiously objectionable material. Plus, it excludes all content posted on the Jewish Sabbath, and if users try to sneak in a search on Saturday, Koogle crashes.[1]

One application that's fun to explore is the International Children's Digital Library. Its visual faceted navigation model lets children search for award-winning books with red covers and imaginary characters, for example. The Library's interface and facet selection are wonderfully creative and may inspire novel ideas in disparate contexts.

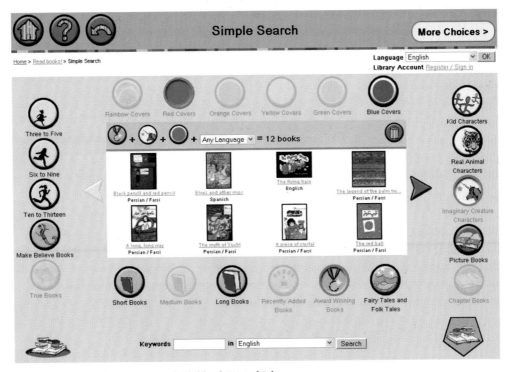

Figure 5-21. *The International Children's Digital Library*

---

1 *"Koogle, a kosher Google, launches,"* Emma Barnett, Telegraph.co.uk (June 15, 2009).

Some applications are designed for professional communities. For instance, ChemSpider is a search engine for chemists. By taking domain expertise for granted, its designers are free to focus on powerful options that include searching by chemical structure, identifier, elements, and properties.

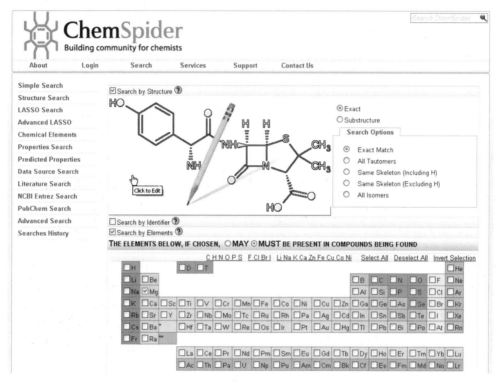

Figure 5-22. *A search engine for chemists*

When developing a specialized application like ChemSpider, it would be a mistake to assume that chemists can search proficiently. We mustn't conflate domain knowledge and search expertise. Whether designing for toddlers or physicists, we'd do well to heed that amazing engine of discovery known as Albert Einstein: "Everything should be made as simple as possible, but not simpler."

# PLATFORM

Designers can learn by studying solutions that have been developed for distinct platforms and channels, just as anthropologists benefit by visiting remote islands and mountain villages. Novel adaptations arise in each niche, sometimes in response to unique environmental factors and sometimes simply by chance. Often, these mutations have crossover potential.

Spotlight, the system-wide desktop search for Apple's Mac OS X operating system, doesn't get as close to the promise of personal search as Google Desktop, but it does sport some nice features. The left panel makes it easy to limit queries by date or to search specific places, including servers and shared drives. Plus, Spotlight invites users to browse all images, movies, or documents via a standard list or Cover Flow interface.

Figure 5-23. *Apple's Spotlight search*

The iTunes Store shares some of Spotlight's features, but diverges with respect to results. It's a good example of what Alan Cooper calls a "sovereign posture application." Its expansive presentation of Best Bets for each format in combination with myriad scrollable panels and controls clearly anticipates a big screen and the user's full attention.

**Figure 5-24.** *Apple iTunes Store*

Rather than hiding sort order in a pull-down, its assumption of width and its structured data afford a sort-by-column approach that makes all options visible all the time.

Interactive television presents a different type of big-screen experience. Not only must we accommodate a variety of screen sizes, contrast ratios, and resolutions, but we must support couch potatoes of all ages and aptitudes who sit, stand, or sprawl four to six feet from the set with a remote control as their only input device.

In light of these constraints, large text, oversize controls, autocomplete, autosuggest, and a simple interface are all critical to success. Consider the claims of TiVo executives:

> *What Google did for the Internet, TiVo is now doing for TV, bringing people a combination of excellent search results and innovative discovery that can't be found anywhere else...it works as a discovery engine, helping users find content they didn't even know they can get...[and it incorporates] Amazon Video on Demand and YouTube.*

At present, the Web, albeit with caveats, serves as a pattern library for designers of interactive television. But, undoubtedly, iTV innovations will soon flow the other way.

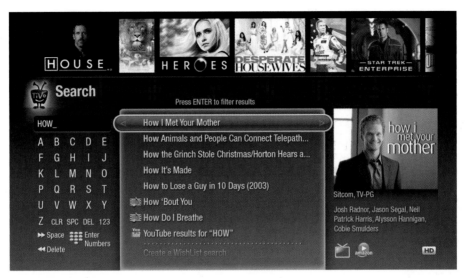

Figure 5-25. *TiVo search*

At the other end of the spectrum, mobile search applications must presume small screens, fat thumbs, and partial attention. Consequently, Google Mobile and Apple's Spotlight for iPhone feature advanced autosuggest, and they limit search result metadata to format, title, and sometimes subtitles such as URL or album name.

Figure 5-26. *Google Mobile and Spotlight for iPhone*

Interestingly, both tackle overlapping subsets of personal search. Google Mobile specializes in web and location-aware local search, but also indexes contacts. In contrast, Spotlight covers all the applications, contacts, communications, and media files on the iPhone, but omits the web and web history. A comparison of various desktop and device search applications reveals major opportunities to innovate in the personal search space.

Meanwhile, kiosks are popping up all over. They're in airports, bookstores, and libraries. We use them to buy groceries and DVDs. Yet, despite their increasing ubiquity, kiosks are unfamiliar terrain for most designers. A bit like the denizens of Papua New Guinea, kiosks are isolated from the mainland and subject to different environmental constraints.

Figure 5-27. *Self-service kiosks*

For instance, kiosks are vulnerable to vandals, so standard mice and keyboards are not smart options for input. Also, kiosks must be immediately attractive, engaging, and usable. The totally public nature of the experience dramatically multiplies the fear factor. Users are terrified of looking stupid in front of strangers (or friends), so the interface must be easy to learn and use.

Kiosks must also foster fast transactions so lines don't form and customers don't leave. For all these reasons, kiosks often omit search. This works fine for Redbox, which provides access to its relatively small and structured catalog of movies via an A–Z index and a "browse by genre" feature. But for larger and more heterogeneous collections, search can't be avoided completely. At Kroger grocery stores, for instance, "search by picture" (which is really a visual "browse by category" feature) is the main way to find items without barcodes, but there is a keyword search facility as the next to last resort. Heaven forbid we are forced to humiliate ourselves by calling an attendant for help in public!

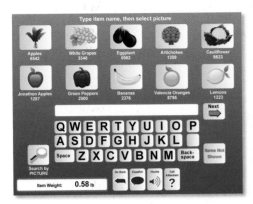 

Figure 5-28. *Kroger and Redbox kiosk interfaces*

# MODE

Sometimes the best way to improve search is to reframe the problem. A search application isn't always the optimal or only path to findability. For this reason, it's worth asking how other information-seeking modes might reinforce or replace search, and it's good to keep an eye on the latest generation of answer engines and discovery tools.

For instance, Aardvark is a "help engine" that employs sophisticated algorithms to route questions to the right people within a user's extended network of friends, friends of friends, classmates, coworkers, and even nearby strangers (Figure 5-29). Users can ask and answer questions via instant messaging, using a website or mobile app, over email, or through Twitter. Most questions are answered in under five minutes. It's good for finding facts and even better for soliciting opinions. By rendering search as a shout, Aardvark taps into people's willingness to help out in small ways, especially when they get to offer advice. In this way, it's not just a search tool; it's a knowledge management innovation.

Hunch, shown in Figure 5-30, is another intriguing example. It's a collective intelligence decision-making system that engages users and software in the collaborative creation and refinement of decision trees. Hunch transforms search into a garden of forking paths where a series of simple questions and answers stimulates learning and discovery. Hunch doesn't just provide interesting answers; it also helps users ask the right questions.

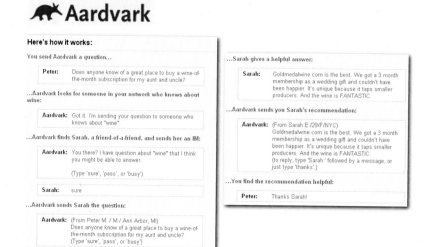

**Figure 5-29.** *Asking questions at Aardvark*

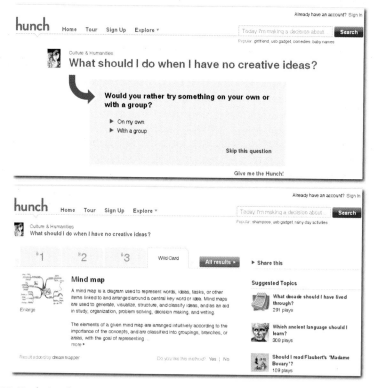

**Figure 5-30.** *Exploring decision space at Hunch*

In contrast, Ambiently serves up answers with no need for questions. From any web page, users simply click a button or bookmarklet to view its Ambient Page, a list of semantically similar or topically related pages. Much like Google's Similar link, Ambiently makes the pearl-growing strategy of experts more easily accessible to all.

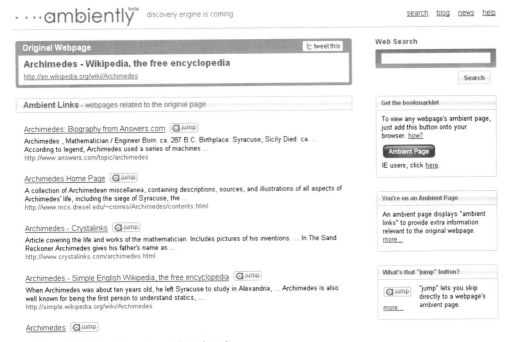

Figure 5-31. *Pearl growing with Ambiently*

Similarly, StumbleUpon requires a click instead of a question. But this serendipity engine is less about the pursuit of relevance than the joy of randomness. StumbleUpon lets users discover and rate web pages, photos, and videos. It employs collaborative filtering and social networking principles to inform recommendations. StumbleUpon reliably serves up amusing or interesting stuff you'd never find through search.

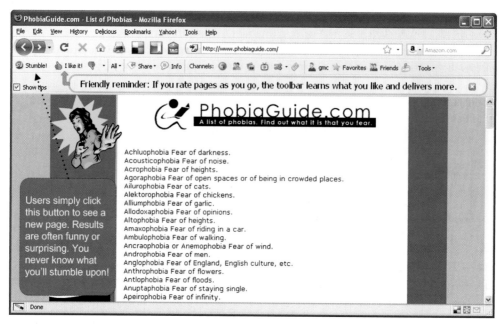

Figure 5-32. *Serendipity with StumbleUpon*

So, each engine strikes a different balance between interestingness and relevance. None delivers the daily sustenance of Google, but each adds a unique twist to the serendipity of search. We must keep fishing for serendipity, because the easy answers have already been caught. As the engines of discovery responsible for inventing tomorrow's search, we must embrace research and development methods that allow us to wonder and wander. We must have the courage to follow the path less traveled and the faith to believe that, as Ovid promised, in the pool where we least expect it, there will be fish.

# 6

# Tangible Futures

*" The wind chime maker invites nature into collaboration. "*
—Brenda Laurel

*Animism* is the belief that souls or spirits exist not only in humans, but also in animals, trees, mountains, rivers, wind, weather, and other natural objects and phenomena. It's an idea that infuses philosophy and religion in countless cultures throughout history. It's also a wellspring for *myths*: traditional stories that explain the origin of the universe, the history of a people, and the purpose of social institutions. One of the main functions of myth is to establish models for behavior. The narratives of Prometheus, Pandora, Sisyphus, Oedipus, and Odysseus are designed to instruct. Our familiarity with these ancient stories proves the power of myth. These lessons endure. They are made to stick.

Interestingly, in modern vernacular, a myth is a false story or belief, but within their cultures of origin, myths are sacred narratives that tell truths about the past. Today, myths have lost credibility, yet they still offer the power of reflection. Through metaphor and analogy, myths reveal the story of ourselves. Heroes, tricksters, and gods are but vessels for the personification of our own hopes and fears. Myths are mirrors. They catalog patterns of experience and expectation. They remind us that what's past is prologue. More than just vivid stories of yesteryear, myths animate and act upon the future.

In design, we would do well to embed similar insight and influence in our deliverables. We need stories and sketches that bring search and discovery to life. We need principles and proverbs that capture the essence of human psychology and behavior. And we need maps and models that shape beliefs about what's possible, probable, and preferable. After all, design is inextricably invested in the future. Our research reveals the latent desire lines that inspire new products, and our prototypes engage people in spirited discussions of strategy, technology, and experience. In an era where the hard things are the soft things, our work invests ideas with substance. We transform abstract patterns and proposals into physical artifacts with sensory and emotional resonance. While our hearts are in the betterment of communication and collaboration, there's no question we're in the business of persuasion. We change minds. Our prototypes and predictions influence the future, even when they're wrong. We are the makers of maps and myths. We are entrusted with the authority to put the soul in search by making tomorrow tangible.

# METHODS AND DELIVERABLES

The design of search is a tricky business. Each project is unique. Restructuring an enterprise intranet, migrating an e-commerce experience to the mobile platform, and inventing a "new to the world" decision engine are clearly sisters of a different order. However, just as patterns of behavior and design transcend category and platform, so do our methods and deliverables. In fact, there's nothing special about search. A standard issue user experience toolbox and a bit of advanced common sense are really all we need.

For starters, we must select research methods that fit the context. Unobtrusive field observation is rarely practical, since search is generally ad hoc. But we can surely draw upon other ethnographic techniques, including interviews, questionnaires, and diary study. Classic usability testing also works well, but it's important to avoid oversimplification. Basic tasks (e.g., try to find) should be interspersed with real-world scenarios. Users must be free to search *and* browse. And it's often useful to ask how people would normally find the answer or solve the problem if not with this specific site or application.

**Figure 6-1.** *The trials of usability*

Search analytics are another obvious choice. For a website, it's useful to compare the most popular internal and external queries. What's the difference between the search terms that deliver people to the site and the queries they perform when they get there? By asking this question, we often expose gaps in marketing and design that we must address by improving both search engine optimization and the site's information architecture. Of course, it's important to recognize the limits of quantitative analysis. The data tells us the terms people use, but not what they seek or whether they succeed. A mix of methods helps us to interpret the data, place anomalies in context, and begin to see the big picture.

For that reason, it's also vital to conduct internal meetings and stakeholder interviews. Since search is a multidisciplinary collaboration of design, engineering, marketing, and management, success requires that we engage participation across departments and units. Conversations should cover mission, vision, strategy, time, budget, human resources, and technology infrastructure. It's also good to ask about metrics for success and models of best practice, since these questions elicit examples that bring discussions down to earth.

During discovery, and especially in these meetings, it's important to turn the observer problem into an opportunity. Simply by being present and asking questions, we exert influence, subtle or not. The right nudges now can avert problems later. Even at this early stage, it's worth visualizing and shaping both journey and destination.

Similarly, we should invert our thinking about deliverables. Our artifacts are not just tools for persuasion; they're also vehicles for exploration. A concept map lets us reframe the problem and elicit a response. A process flow lets us wander the actual and possible paths of users in search of shortcuts and serendipity. Prototypes afford the amazing opportunity to create, play with, and learn from tangible products of the imagination. We should heed the invitation of Figure 6-2 to lay out all our deliverables in one place so we can see them in context, consider their purpose, and enjoy the experience of discovery.[1]

*Figure 6-2. User experience deliverables*

---

1 For more on this topic, see "User Experience Deliverables," by Peter Morville and Jeffery Callender, available at *http://semanticstudios.com/publications/semantics/000228.php.*

# SEARCH SCENARIOS

So, in the spirit of play, we propose to explore the future of search and discovery through a series of scenarios. Our aim is not to predict but to persuade and provoke. As a result, our sketches and stories are divergent by design. We'll wander in time and format from images of distant futurity to narratives that could take place tomorrow. As a group, our scenarios won't cohere. But individually, like myths, we hope they stick. We want to inspire you to take risks by taking a few ourselves.

And now for something completely different.…

## SENSORIUM

Anja felt happy. She was sitting cross-legged on Claire's bed. She stole a last glance at the sun-dappled meadow before her best friend drew the curtains and collapsed into a giant pink bean bag in the far corner of the room. Of course, "happy" wasn't the right word, but "elated" was over the top. "Playful" was good. She added "peppy" and "perky" to the query, then "pink" just for fun. Both girls laughed as the results tickled their senses. Images of bunny rabbits and puppy dogs spun into sight. A flock of butterflies flew by overhead. The warble of a barn swallow became a mountain stream, a flute, chimes in the wind.

Claire reached for the sensory controls, nudging up taste and smell, while tapping the soothing tag near the barn swallow icon. The girls sighed in sync as hot chocolate infused with hints of cinnamon and vanilla soothed their preteen limbic systems.

Anja spun the *similar sensewheel* and landed on s'mores, closing her eyes to savor the crunchy, chocolatey, smoky, sticky mess. A soft sob broke the spell. Anja looked up to see her friend in tears. Claire replied to the query on Anja's face with, "I miss my mom."

Claire's mom had died the year before. The brain cancer was detected early, but it was too deep for surgery and unresponsive to drugs and radiation. That's why the girls didn't visit much anymore. Claire's dad had moved to the country to "get away from it all." Whatever that meant. They still hung out virtually every day, but it wasn't the same as in person.

Claire sat quietly in the corner in her big pink bean bag.

"Show me," Anja whispered.

Claire summoned a video wall with her left hand, her fingers and eyes dancing their way through a colorful montage of bedtime stories, birthday parties, sing-alongs, and other bittersweet memories that started sad but trended too quickly to sunlight and sugar.

"No," said Anja softly, looking directly into her friend's eyes. "Show me."

Claire stared back for a moment, took a deep breath, then flipped the switch for emotive output. Anja gasped as feelings of loss, fear, anger, and guilt washed through her medial temporal lobes. She closed her eyes and covered her ears, but couldn't shut out the pain. She felt like weeping and wailing and tearing her own flesh. The sensations of darkness and despair were unbearable, consuming, neverending. And then they were gone.

Claire joined Anja on the bed, and the two friends embraced. After tears had run their course, Claire caught Anja's eye and conjured a rainbow that lit up the room. Anja responded with a flag waving in the wind. It was red, white, and pink. The game began anew. The girls searched and stumbled and smiled through their five senses and beyond.

Anja soon felt happy. Of course, happy wasn't exactly the right word.

## DEBRIEF

A real sci-fi writer wouldn't deign to explain the story and probably wouldn't need to. But we dilettantes may add value by debriefing, especially when the tale is but a catalyst for conversation. In our flash fiction, we imagine a game of search in a world where neural implants afford direct sensory input and output. Queries and results can be rendered by touch, taste, sight, sound, or smell. Our matrix of hardware and wetware even enables the direct or indirect exchange of raw emotion. It's a radical proposition, but not necessarily impossible and certainly not unimaginable. What could this future mean for search? What types of interfaces and interactions can we envision?

Feels like...     Tastes like...     Looks like...     Sounds like...     Smells like...

Figure 6-3. *Multisensory search*

For starters, words will take us only so far. Perhaps the act or memory of sensing will form the query. Pearl growing and incremental construction—like that, but a bit more of this—will be vital. Progressive disclosure will guide the presentation of multiformat results by fading less popular senses into background options. Indeed, many people may enjoy the opportunity to try the cross-sensory experience of synesthesia, but we'll need to employ our scented widgets, flavorful facets, and sonic snippets judiciously to prevent pogosticking ad nauseam. *Don't Make Me Sick* might be Steve Krug's next bestseller.

A good scenario doesn't just provoke us to ponder the future; it changes how we think about today. Sensorium might, for instance, spur new ideas about stock photography.

Figure 6-4. *Happy at Corbis*

Are keywords and controlled vocabularies really the best we can do? Or can we transcend the limits of language? Automatic pattern recognition is one option. Software that scans facial expressions to derive emotions shows real promise. But what else? What's next?

## SEMANTIC SINGULARITY

The entertainment system was belting out the Beatles'"Let It Be" when the iPhone rang. When Pete answered, his phone turned down the sound by messaging all nearby devices with a volume control. Lucy, his sister's agent, was on the line. "Mom's at the hospital. She had chest pain. The doctors ran tests and established a diagnosis of...." Lucy was cut off by Hugh, Pete's agent, who appeared as a hologram on the table nearby.

"Hey Pete, I've bought you three pairs of running shoes, Nike+ LunarGlides, top of the line. I'm wearing a pair. Check 'em out."

"Hold on!" shouted Pete. "I'm on the phone with Lucy. Lucy, are you there? What's wrong with Mom?" Lucy explained that Mom had an episode of angina. "She's stable and should be fine. Jenny's taking her home." Pete promised to meet his mom and sister there soon, then turned his attention to Hugh. "So, what's up with the Nikes?"

"Heart disease is hereditary," replied Hugh. "You already have most of the risk factors. You're male, inactive, and overweight. You drink too much. Your blood pressure and cholesterol are high. You're getting older. Plus, you're under stress. Your mom's diagnosis pushed you from alert level orange to red: severe risk of heart attack. I've put together an exercise program. We'll be running five days a week. Also, I've consulted with your doctor's agent. You'll be taking 80mg of Lipitor daily, starting tomorrow."

Before Pete could argue, the doorbell rang and the fire alarm went off. He dashed into the kitchen, jerked the smoking pan of Chef Boyardee beef ravioli off the burner (apparently his phone had turned down the volume on his stopwatch), silenced the alarm, and ran to the front door. He was greeted by a teenage girl wearing a green striped uniform. "Delivery. Prepaid. Butternut squash in coconut milk with tofu and toasted almonds." She handed him a box, warm and damp on the bottom, and left with a wave.

"What the hell is this?" Pete demanded back inside.

"Butternut squash," replied Hugh. "It's healthier than pizza. And we had a coupon."

"But I don't like squash. And I didn't order pizza!"

"You swoogled for 'pizza' a half-hour ago. And you opted into that no-click ordering program last week. I did an *autosuggest override* and selected a heart-healthy option."

"I was searching for 'pisa,' not 'pizza.' I'd like to see the tower before it falls."

Hugh defended the autocorrect as statistically valid. He then presented a dynamic, three-dimensional fly-through visualization. "It's a personalized decision matrix," he explained. "Clearly, you've gotta run, go vegan, and take Lipitor. It's your only hope." Finally, he recommended a great hotel in Barcelona, and LightLife veggie burgers.

Pete couldn't grok the data. He'd have to trust Hugh's interpretation. But he wanted to visit Pisa, not Barcelona. And there was no way he was eating veggie burgers. "I'm leaving for Mom's now. I'd like a large pepperoni pizza delivered to her house. Please cancel that shoe order. And disable your autosuggest override function, at least for now. I'm not changing my whole lifestyle just yet, and neither are you."

Hugh shook his head. "I'm sorry, Pete, but you're asking me to violate laws one and three. I can't allow you to come to harm, and I must protect my own existence."

Pete stared at Hugh in astonishment. Things were starting to get creepy. Then he noticed something. His eyes narrowed. "What's that on your bow tie?"

"It's nothing," answered Hugh.

And it was nothing. Just a plain black bow tie. Pete stomped out of the apartment. His car was waiting in the lot, engine running, top down, radio on, door open. As the car drove off, Pete muttered to himself, "I could have sworn there was a logo on that bow tie…."

## DEBRIEF

This scenario is a parody. It mocks "The Semantic Web" by Tim Berners-Lee et al. (*Scientific American*, May 2001). It also pokes fun at Ray Kurzweil's *The Singularity Is Near* (Viking Adult) and Apple Computer's "Knowledge Navigator." These works were authored by brilliant people. They advanced groundbreaking insights and ideas, but they all failed spectacularly to predict the future of human-computer interaction (so far).

While artificial intelligence lies behind each vision, search is often the killer application. The idea that software agents will answer our questions (sometimes before we ask) via a conversational interface is seductive. We also love to imagine an orderly world of co-operative systems and appliances. But life and language are messy. Crosswalking for meaning across vocabularies and standards is difficult, if not impossible. Then there's the trouble with trust; the smarter the agents, the harder they are to trust.

In this scenario, the agents possess a scary level of control. Even when they're not actively making decisions and performing tasks, the agents control access to information. Their alerts, algorithms, and filters influence which facts are found and whose opinions come first. And they just might be working for someone else, or for themselves.

LET ME REMIND YOU OF ASIMOV'S THREE LAWS:

1. A ROBOT MAY NOT INJURE A HUMAN BEING OR, THROUGH INACTION, ALLOW A HUMAN BEING TO COME TO HARM.

2. A ROBOT MUST OBEY ANY ORDERS GIVEN TO IT BY HUMAN BEINGS, EXCEPT WHERE SUCH ORDERS WOULD CONFLICT WITH THE FIRST LAW.

3. A ROBOT MUST PROTECT ITS OWN EXISTENCE AS LONG AS SUCH PROTECTION DOES NOT CONFLICT WITH THE FIRST OR SECOND LAW.

OF COURSE, THESE ARE ALL SUBJECT TO (MY) INTERPRETATION...

Figure 6-5. *A semantic agent*

Of course, it may be premature to question the ethics and motives of our agents. While it's cool that WolframAlpha can answer a few big questions, in truth, semantic search hasn't progressed much beyond parlor tricks. Software can extract a little more meaning from natural language texts and questions by parsing sentences for actor-action-object triples, but simple keyword queries generally remain the most efficient way to start.

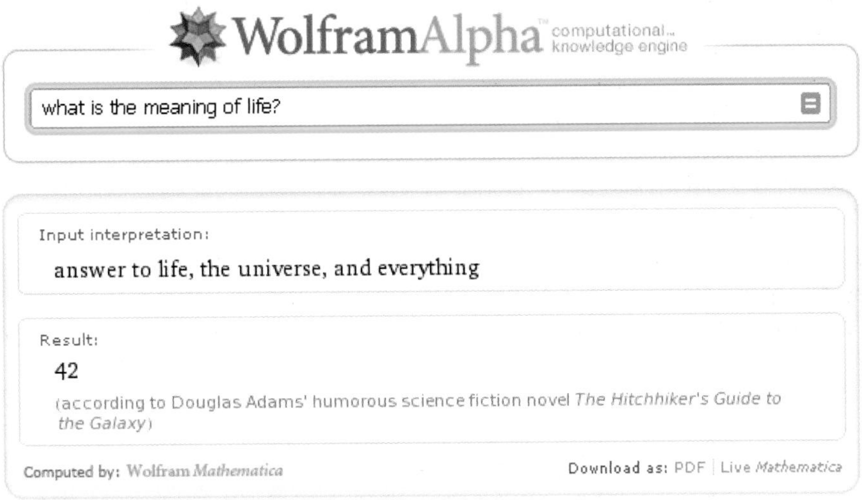

Figure 6-6. *The answer from WolframAlpha*

There's a big gap between the claims of semantic search companies and the performance of their products. Consider, for instance, this excerpt from Cognition's website:

> *Cognition's natural language technology employs a unique mix of linguistics and mathematical algorithms which has, in effect, taught the computer the meanings (or associated concepts) of nearly all the words and frequently used phrases within the common English language. It also has knowledge of the relations between words and phrases, especially paraphrase (a 'finger' or a 'digit') and taxonomy (a 'finger' is part of a 'hand', a 'cow' is a 'bovine' and is a 'mammal').* [2]

Cognition goes on to explain that its software "understands the meaning within the context of the text it is processing." So, why can't it figure out that a user who asks, "Where is Java?" is probably looking for a place, not a programming language? (To its credit, WolframAlpha nails this one, serving up a link to Java Island and a map of Indonesia, which is great provided you're not looking for Java, South Dakota.)

---

2 *www.cognition.com/info/what.html*

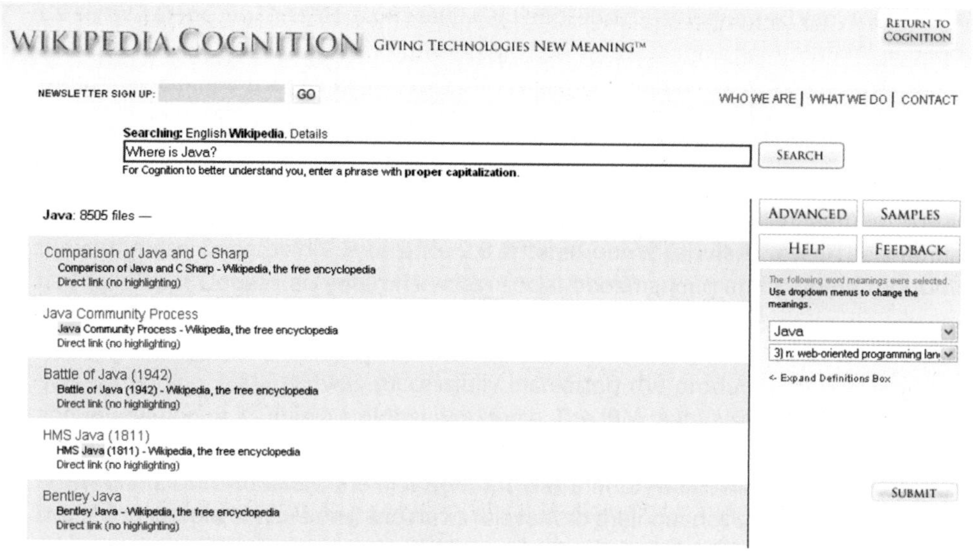

Figure 6-7. *Searching for Java with Cognition*

It's not that there's no value in parsing sentences for meaning or developing thesauri (or ontologies) that map equivalent, hierarchical, and associative relationships. These approaches can add value, especially within verticals with limited, formal vocabularies like medicine, law, and engineering. It's just that less obvious approaches—like employing query-query reformulation and post-query click data to drive autosuggest—may deliver better results at lower cost. And we should be wary of claims that computers "understand meaning," at least until they get a whole lot better at filtering spam.

But we don't need the future to worry about trust. Google already shapes what we find, learn, and believe. And Google isn't transparent; it is a multibillion-dollar company that earns nearly all its revenue from advertising and maintains its ranking algorithm as a closely held trade secret. Google knows more about us than we know about Google. Google claims that because of personalization, the more we share, the better the results. How do we know we can trust Google? Is "Don't be evil" enough? Should we continue to search and share in good faith? Or is evil subject to interpretation? Is it possible that personalization is more about targeted advertising than relevant results? However we answer these questions, the fact is that ranking algorithms are an invisible yet powerful force in our lives. Their power will only grow. What about their visibility?

## SEARCHVALENCE

Jen realized she'd lost Bruce when she found his iGlasses on a shelf in a used bookstore on Castro Street. They'd planned to meet up after her walk through Golden Gate Park. But now what? He could be anywhere. Deciding she'd rather spend a little money than a lot of time, Jen fired up Google's PeopleFinder.

Jen opted for all pattern recognition methods and set the search area at a square mile.

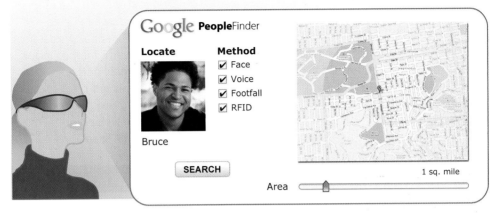

Fortunately, Bruce wasn't sleeping in the park like last time. A camera picked him up near Frederick and Stanyan.

Jen approved the task budget, and Mechanical Turk found a worker nearby. Bruce agreed to meet back at the bookstore.

Figure 6-8. *Searchvalence*

## DEBRIEF

In urban environments, we're already surrounded by video cameras, some integrated with microphone surveillance systems that can recognize a discrete sound, identify the point of origin, and turn cameras to focus precisely on that location. Imagine these cameras networked and their streaming video and audio available to the public for a fee. Now add iGlasses with Life Caching A/V worn by everyone who's anyone, and a layer of sophisticated face and voice recognition software. Maybe we'll have smart sidewalks and floors to track people by their unique footfall signatures. And don't forget the radio-frequency identification (RFID) tags in our wallets, shoes, and underwear—and perhaps a *FriendChip*™ or two under our skin.

Sure, this prospect may seem a bit spooky, but it's worth thinking through some of the intriguing possibilities. For instance, what if we could watch and listen through another's eyes and ears, assuming they gave us permission? This is already happening in a crude way. Just watch all the cellphones held high during an Olympic Opening Ceremony. And don't forget the life cache—we'll be able to see and hear history in the making, for a price. Designing search for this scenario should be interesting, especially since the best insights may emerge from the collective motion and behavior of crowds.

## FLOCK

Paul was looking forward to a late lunch with his three girls. The Black Sheep's turkey club was awesome, and the girls said the Grandma Cake was to die for. And, as Bing had predicted, the deli was quiet this afternoon. Before they could grab a table, Paul's mobile beeped. It was a SIQ alert.

Bing had identified a cluster of statistically improbable queries issued by people who'd recently been in this location.

Outside the deli, Paul tried to calm the kids while figuring out Plan B. He scanned tomorrow's query forecast for ideas.

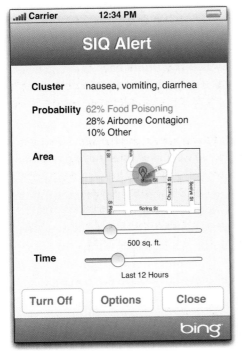

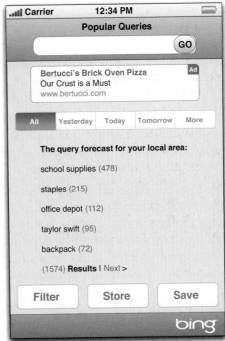

"School starts next week. Let's grab a burger at Blimpy's, and then buy supplies next door, before the big rush," said Paul.

Unfortunately, he wasn't the only one ahead of the curve.

Figure 6-9. *Flock*

## DEBRIEF

Imagine you're sitting on a plane when the captain announces (without explanation) an indefinite ground stop on all inbound and outbound aircraft. Or you're sitting on the grass in Central Park when a jumbo jet pursued by two F-16 fighters flies low over downtown Manhattan. How do you learn what's going on? If it's a major event, CNN will pick it up eventually. But what about right now? Increasingly, a real-time search on Twitter is the fastest (albeit not the most authoritative) source of information.

It's not hard to foresee that we'll soon be relying on data about what people are saying, doing, and searching for—right now—to influence our own actions, decisions, and destinations. Google is already able to predict over half of the most popular queries in a 12-month forecast with a mean absolute prediction error of 12 percent.[3] Add location and personalization, and you've got an excellent baseline for identifying interesting new trends and deviations from the norm.

Clearly, real-time access to social activity metrics might alert us to news before it's news. It might also help us find the most popular nightclub or the fastest route through rush hour. Of course, we'll have to endure accidental flash mobs, as everyone spontaneously and simultaneously decides to visit the same unusually quiet café. We may have to pay good money for access to the best predictive algorithms and social signifiers, but this capability could add sense and shape to our collective (and individual) behavior.

# EXPERIENCE DISCOVERY

These search scenarios are simple tools for engaging people in thought and conversation about possible and preferable futures. We can explore more sophisticated artifacts on video-sharing sites, such as YouTube, which overflow with prototypes and provocations concerning the future of food, communication, learning, health, cars, kitchens, mobile devices, and the Web. As experience designers, we have a wide spectrum of hot and cold media from which to fashion our images of the future. We may employ the logic and order of a formal presentation to persuade one audience while relying on the nonlinear nature of a preliminary sketch to draw a different audience into participatory design.

This diversity of formats is among the reasons we're seeing convergence in the practices of futures studies and experience design. Futurists and forecasters understand the degree to which the impact of what we say is influenced by how we say it. In fact, Jason Tester of the Institute for the Future argues for a new discipline of Human-Future Interaction (HFI) that integrates futures thinking with the methods and deliverables of HCI. He defines HFI as "the art and science of effectively and ethically communicating research, forecasts, and scenarios about trends and potential futures,"[4] and notes the importance of user testing and rapid, iterative prototyping. Jason explains that "a

---

3 *http://googleresearch.blogspot.com/2009/08/on-predictability-of-search-trends.html*

4 "The case for human-future interaction," by Jason Tester, available at *http://future.iftf.org/2007/02/the_case_for_hu.html.*

growing view of the future as a medium that anyone can affect and co-create" means this work has value and resonance far beyond the walls of traditional think tanks and forecasting groups.

As designers, we've always had one foot in the future, but in search and discovery the pace of innovation is forcing us to jump head first. Consider augmented reality (AR), for example. Until recently, mainstream AR was limited to the yellow "first down" line in television broadcasts of American football. But now AR applications like Wikitude, Layar, and Yelp's Monocle are flourishing on Android mobiles and the iPhone 3GS.

Figure 6-10. *Yelp Monocle and Metro Paris Subway*

While early adopters may be frustrated by problems with technology, design, and data quality, this ability to overlay information on the real-time camera view by using the GPS, compass, and accelerometer to determine location and direction is clearly a game changer for mobile search and discovery. All we need now is the heads-up display!

Of course, we have much work ahead: uncovering valuable use cases, identifying successful design patterns, and defining a vocabulary for talking about mixed reality that encompasses both augmented reality and augmented virtuality (the merging of real-world objects into virtual worlds). Since we can't rely on the old desktop metaphor, we must invent new idioms for communication and interaction. Already, we're seeing terms like "magic lens" and "enchanted window" to describe AR, which suggests that Mike Kuniavsky and Brenda Laurel are ahead of the game.

For several years, Kuniavsky has been an advocate for what he calls the coming age of magic:

> *I mean enchanted objects. What I'm proposing is a metaphorical relationship between magic and portable, network-aware, information processing objects that is analogous to the relationship between office supplies and computer screens in the desktop metaphor. I am explicitly not advocating pretending that technology is a kind of magic or lying about how technology works, but using our existing cultural understanding of magic objects as an abstraction to describe the behavior of ubiquitous computing devices.* [5]

He notes that what differentiates enchanted objects is "their ability to have independent behaviors, to communicate, to remember, and to interact with other enchanted objects and people" without screens or keyboards. Magic as a metaphor, Kuniavsky argues, is an emergent, familiar pattern that transcends culture, material, and context.

In similar fashion, Laurel has advanced the concept of "designed animism" as a way of framing our relationship with objects in wireless sensor networks:

> *Sensors that gather information about wind, or solar flares, or neutrino showers, or bird migrations, or tides, or processes inside a living being, or dynamics of an ecosystem are means by which designers can invite nature into collaboration, and the invisible patterns they capture can be brought into the realm of the senses in myriad new ways.* [6]

She suggests that by marrying animism with a sense of poetics, we can tap the affordances of ambient computing to invent new forms of pleasurable experience. We can change the world through delight. It's an intriguing vision that encourages us to weave elements of magic, myth, emotion, and empathy into the tapestry of our future.

Fortunately, we can't predict the future. We can barely forecast the weather. To pretend otherwise is an act of hubris, the greatest sin in the eyes of the ancient gods. It's this uncertainty that makes Horace's lyric poetry both tempting and timeless: *Carpe diem quam minimum credula postero*, or "Seize the day; trust tomorrow as little as you may."

Delightfully, there's no shortage of problems with search today. Even as we speculate about the Future with a capital F, Google is quietly figuring out how to disambiguate GM (General Motors or genetically modified). For every unsolved problem, there are countless instances in which we know the solution, but nobody has bothered to implement it. Discipline and attention to detail would go a long way toward improving the world of search. A heads-down focus on the tasks of today can often produce both pleasure and progress.

---

5 "The Coming Age of Magic," by Mike Kuniavsky, available at *www.orangecone.com/tm_etech_magic_0.3.pdf*.

6 "Designed Animism," by Brenda Laurel, available at *www.tauzero.com/Brenda_Laurel/DesignedAnimism/DesignedAnimism.html*.

But we'd be remiss in our responsibility if we ignore the shadow of the future. We're not simply in the business of designing experiences. We must also grasp the curious, collaborative challenge of experience discovery. By investing in exploratory research and experimental design, we can work with our users to discover and cocreate new products, inventive applications, and desirable experiences. This will require insight and foresight.

To make search better, we must embrace the genius of the AND. We must look to the center and the periphery. We must learn from fact and fiction. We must use compelling stories and colorful artifacts as our microscopes, telescopes, and kaleidoscopes. It's not sufficient to adopt and adapt patterns. We must innovate. We must bring search to life. To accomplish these lofty goals, we must entertain both the present and the future.

Figure 6-11. *The butterfly effect*

In this adventure, we might employ the butterfly effect as a metaphorical bridge between tomorrow and today. The term derives from a short sci-fi story by Ray Bradbury in which a hunter from 2055 travels into the past on a prehistoric safari, accidentally kills a butterfly, and returns to find his present has been changed in subtle yet meaningful ways. The phrase was given new life by Edward Lorenz, a mathematician and meteorologist who pioneered chaos theory by discovering how sensitive dependence on initial conditions shapes weather patterns. He's credited with the aphorism that the flap of a butterfly's wings in Brazil could set off a tornado in Texas.[7] This fact, that little things make a big difference, governs all complex systems, and it certainly applies to search.

Our work helps people find the products, places, and information they need, and the data that makes a difference. As designers of applications for search and discovery, we shape the future of learning and literacy. Search plays a vital role in the curation of knowledge and the provocation of creativity. It's poised to engage our senses and lift our spirits in ways we can barely imagine. It's a topic both timely and timeless. Search is a core life activity, as ancient in its form as the trees and hills, and as our faces are. We must discover its patterns, and break them with intent. Let's get flapping!

---

7 Due to Edward Lorenz's discovery of strange attractors, their visual representation, which illustrates order underlying chaos (pictured in Figure 6-11), is known as a *Lorenz butterfly*.

# Recommended Reading

# Index

# ABOUT THE AUTHORS

**Peter Morville** is best known as a founder of the field of information architecture. His bestselling books include *Information Architecture for the World Wide Web* and *Ambient Findability* (both O'Reilly). He advises such clients as AT&T, Harvard, IBM, the Library of Congress, Microsoft, the National Cancer Institute, Vodafone, and the Weather Channel; and delivers keynotes and workshops at conferences around the world. His pioneering work on experience strategy and the future of search has been covered by *Business Week*, the *Economist*, *Fortune*, NPR, and the *Wall Street Journal*. Peter lives in Ann Arbor, Michigan, with his wife, two daughters, and a dog named Knowsy. You can reach him by email at *morville@semanticstudios.com*. You can also find him online at *semanticstudios.com*, *findability.org*, and *searchpatterns.org*.

**Jeff Callender** is vice president and design director of Q LTD, a strategic design consultancy with a global reach. Jeff is focused on bringing clarity to everyday graphic communications that promote positive user experiences. His wide body of work includes design for brand identity, user interface, print collateral, packaging, tradeshow, and exhibit graphics for a variety of clients including AT&T, Converse, Dow, NuStep, Jensen, ProQuest, and SIGGRAPH. Jeff has taught graphic design at the University of Michigan and lectured at its Stephen M. Ross School of Business and the SIGGRAPH Conference on Computer Graphics and Interactive Techniques.

# COLOPHON

The image on the cover of *Search Patterns* is a *Charaxes brutus*, or white-barred charaxes, a butterfly of the *Nymphalidae* family. Native to Africa, the white-barred charaxes is a favorite of collectors due to the intricate, colorful patterns on the undersides of its wings. The butterfly is black with a broad white band on both sides of its wings, as its name implies.

Aided by a large wingspan of 8–10 centimeters, *Charaxes brutus* is one of the fastest butterflies in the world, capable of reaching speeds of up to 40 miles per hour. Its speed, coupled with the fact that it prefers densely wooded areas and flies high in the tree canopy, has traditionally made it a difficult species to catch.

In Africa, harvesting wild butterflies is a lucrative field; profits from a rare specimen can support an entire family. Using screen traps with baits of dung and fermented fruit, harvesters can lure this elusive butterfly to them and entrap it. While mounted specimens are commercially available, butterfly conservancies afford people the opportunity to view this impressive species live.

The cover image is from the Dover Pictorial Archive. The cover font is Adobe ITC Garamond. The text and heading font is Myriad Pro.

# Buy this book and get access to the online edition for 45 days—for free!

*Design for Discovery*

# Search Patterns

O'REILLY®  *Peter Morville & Jeffery Callender*

**Search Patterns**

By Peter Morville & Jeffery Callender
January 2010, $39.99
ISBN 9780596802271

## With Safari Books Online, you can:

**Access the contents of thousands of technology and business books**

- Quickly search over 7000 books and certification guides
- Download whole books or chapters in PDF format, at no extra cost, to print or read on the go
- Copy and paste code
- Save up to 35% on O'Reilly print books
- **New!** Access mobile-friendly books directly from cell phones and mobile devices

**Stay up-to-date on emerging topics before the books are published**

- Get on-demand access to evolving manuscripts.
- Interact directly with authors of upcoming books

**Explore thousands of hours of video on technology and design topics**

- Learn from expert video tutorials
- Watch and replay recorded conference sessions

To try out Safari and the online edition of this book FREE for 45 days, go to **www.oreilly.com/go/safarienabled** and enter the coupon code BXLOJFH. To see the complete Safari Library, visit safari.oreilly.com.

Spreading the knowledge of innovators

safari.oreilly.com